LOOK
WHO'S
TALKING!

LOOK WHO'S TALKING!

A Guide for Lay Speakers in the Church

Ronald E. Sleeth

ABINGDON PRESS   NASHVILLE

LOOK WHO'S TALKING!

Library of Congress Cataloging in Publication Data

SLEETH, RONALD EUGENE.
  Look who's talking!
  1. Public speaking. I. Title.
PN4121.S486   808.5′1   77-1171

ISBN 0-687-22630-9

MANUFACTURED BY THE PARTHENON PRESS AT
NASHVILLE, TENNESSEE, UNITED STATES OF AMERICA

For
John C. Irwin
and
David C. Shipley

There was something about this man
that gave me the conviction that we
could approach ultimates together.

Saul Bellow, *Henderson the Rain King*

Introduction

Look Who's Talking rests upon certain assumptions. For one thing, it is addressed primarily to lay persons. We have been told that this is the day of the laity, but the lay person has few places to turn to get competent help in communicating his or her faith to others.

The future of the church may well depend upon men and women who can communicate effectively. No matter how competent the clergy, they cannot do it alone. Indeed, it is not their responsibility to do so. God's people are all members of Christ's Body—the church—and all are bearers of the Word.

More importantly, all of us need to know how to articulate our faith. In fact, it might be said that a belief is not a belief until we can speak about it. Many Christians have vague ideas or feelings about the faith, but until they are asked to stand on their feet and speak, those beliefs may not be clear. Speaking about them brings them alive.

It is also apparent that all of us as church men and women are called upon to perform a variety of leadership roles that depend upon effective communication. This book addresses some of those situations and takes the mystery out of them.

Finally, human speech is one of the greatest of God's gifts. *Look Who's Talking* makes the primary claim that speech is the main link of communication among humans. To communicate with another effectively is as noble as it is necessary.

The book itself was born on a plane between El Paso and Dallas, Texas, when Dr. Richard S. Smith of the Methodist Board of Discipleship suggested that I write a book on basic communication for lay persons. We had been on the staff of a lay speakers' conference for the lay persons of New Mexico, and both of us had felt the need for more adequate resources to train lay speakers. Dr. Smith has been most helpful at every point along the way. Appreciation should also be expressed to Mrs. Mary Ann Marshall of Perkins School of Theology, who typed the bulk of the manuscript, and Mrs. Wilma Bizaro of West Virginia Wesleyan College, who assisted with the final corrections.

Contents

LOOK
WHO'S
TALKING!

1

Speech Is a "Cool" Medium
(Principles of Communication)

Human speech is a wonderful gift! Indeed, spoken language sets us off from all other creatures in God's universe. Words expressed orally remain the basic means of communication among humans. As Susanne Langer has said, "The fact is that our primary world of reality *is* a verbal one."

Whether we are simply saying "Good morning" or are witnessing to our faith, the words we speak are the means of joining two or more persons in communion. These words do not simply flesh out our thoughts; they also reveal who we are.

be careful little tongue

Occasionally in our day we hear criticisms of speaking. There are simply too many words being uttered by politicians, preachers, and commercial hucksters. We all need to stop talking so much and listen more. And, we do need to be aware of other persons' ideas and feelings. But stopping talk altogether would not solve those problems. That would keep us from communicating. We all need to have a better idea of what communication is, and then we need to become more skilled at it. Words, language, and speech combine to make us human and to make us communicators.

Other critics contend that speech is overrated because so much of our communication is nonverbal. We communicate with our eyes, faces, gestures, and feeling tone. Words get overemphasized, they claim, because real meaning is not transmitted verbally. Again, it is true that much of what gets communicated is more, or deeper, than words. Our faces may reveal attitudes that support or oppose what we say. A preacher may be preaching on love, but the lines around his eyes may reveal hate or anger. A politician may spout slogans about the impoverished persons of our land, yet his manner may reveal a lack of compassion. In both cases, it is not the fault of the words but the manner. Such persons are communicating improperly. In short, what is often called nonverbal communication is no such thing. Ours is a verbal world.

Some people use the word *nonverbal* when they really mean *nonvocal*. We might say that a stoplight communicates nonverbally because we stop on the color red without seeing or thinking the word. Yet the color red, in this case, is based on a verbal utterance—Stop. The nonverbal symbols are normally derivatives of speech; they are simply not vocalized. Even deaf children are taught to speak; they use a sign language that is based upon spoken words. One communication expert, Frank Dance, has said that the old saying "A picture is worth ten thousand words" is only true if we know what the ten thousand words are before we see the picture. Not all of our language is vocal; but it is verbal at its heart. When a person goes to a psychiatrist for therapy, he or she "talks it out." Even at the deepest emotional level there is a correlation between language and feelings.

For the Christian, the idea that speech is the basis of human communication comes as no surprise. "Tell me the old, old,

14

story" has long been on the lips of Christians asking for instruction in their faith. "And God *said*" introduces the acts of creation. He spoke, and the world came into being. One of God's greatest gifts to Adam was allowing his participation in the creative act by naming all of the animals. The prophets spoke forth in the name of God. Jesus came as the Word made flesh; he taught in parables and *spoke* to the multitudes. After his death and resurrection, the early apostles "came preaching" the good news of Christ. Whether referred to as heralds, ambassadors, witnesses, apostles, or preachers, the church has always depended upon the spoken word to carry her message.

Many of the greatest of the early church leaders were those who had been trained in schools of rhetoric and then used those skills of communication to spread the gospel. In the fourth century particularly, when Christianity had grown to a respectable acceptance in the Graeco-Roman world, the leaders were those who were competent in rhetoric, and they "baptized" the work of Aristotle, Quintillian, Cicero, and others to be used in the service of God. In the Eastern church, Basil the Great, Gregory of Nazianzus, Gregory of Nyssa, and Chrysostom were all trained in rhetoric. The same was true in the West for Augustine, who wrote a book of Christian rhetoric.

Years before Christ, rhetoric was a subject studied and practiced by such men as Aristotle and Demosthenes. Schools of rhetoric were prevalent when the gospel came into being. Some may still sneer at rhetoric and call it evil because the techniques can be used for manipulation as well as communication, but the schools of rhetoric that flourished

15

before the time of Christ and continued throughout the centuries were in fact comparable to our colleges. Rhetoric was a discipline of the liberal arts, a course of study designed to provide students with the broad background of knowledge needed for practicing law, politics, and (later) the Christian ministry.

At the time of Christ, and particularly as the gospel moved into the larger world of the Greeks and Romans, those who were trained in the art of communication were converted. Paul was undoubtedly aware of the schools of rhetoric, and some believe his epistles, and particularly his speech on Mars Hill at Athens, are examples of his rhetorical influence. In any event, the Christian gospel (which derived from the Jewish heritage of prophetic utterance and synagogue preaching) joined with secular learning concerning communication to become the means of spreading the gospel throughout the known world.

Later the Reformers based their theology upon the doctrine of the Word of God. It was a Word to be spoken; indeed, one confession went so far as to state that the "preaching of the Word of God *is* the Word of God." In any event, the Christian tradition—both Catholic and Protestant—has affirmed that the good news of the Gospel has been entrusted to the mouths of her ministers and priests. Although the message comes from the Bible and is conserved in the church, it is handed on person to person by word of mouth. A modern theologian Gerhard Ebeling affirms, "If the word of faith—which the New Testament calls the Gospel—had not reached us this way, by word of mouth, by being passed on personally, then we should know nothing about faith."

16

So, when the Christian hears the word that is espoused by communication theorists that ours is a verbal society, he or she nods affirmatively. The whole biblical history of faith including the good news of Christ has been entrusted to the sound of human voice. Word, language, and speech are part and parcel of proclaiming the revelation of God to man. The resurgence of interest in the narrative, story, metaphor, and language points to the continuing interest in bringing the gospel alive in human speech. Luther once stated that "the Church is not a pen-house but a mouth-house." Those who witness to the gospel—whether lay or clergy—affirm that statement and then equip themselves to be worthy witnesses.

We see, then, that ours is a society held together by language, words, and speech. But, speaking should not be like shooting arrows into the air. It should not be like shouting at a soundproof wall. Speech in human communication needs a receiver, a responder, another person or persons. Indeed, there are those who define communication as simply and precisely as that. Dance contends that "human communication is the eliciting of a response through verbal symbols." We speak in order to make ourselves understood, but also to reach another and get a response from that person or persons. In communicating we are trying to affect or influence another. In speaking to a group, and often to a single person, we are attempting to elicit a specific response. Even broadly speaking, communication is seeking a response. As suggested earlier, a casual "Good morning" communicates something and ties people together. More than that, though, a response is sought. A grumpy nod, a smile, or another "Good morning" is a response to that greeting.

If secular communicators from Aristotle to Dance contend that human communication seeks a response, intends to affect others, and tries to persuade, then Christians need not be bashful about their interest in persuading, witnessing, and influencing others through the gospel. Speech is not just the way we relate to one another; it is also the way we influence one another.

Persuasion makes us nervous because we have had high-pressure salesmen or slick con artists or even an occasional smooth-talking preacher try to manipulate us. Yet so many tools of speech like persuasion are perfectly neutral and can be used for good or ill.

One of the ways we can see the difference between the persuader and the manipulator is to understand the distinction between *authority* and *advocacy*. Jesus spoke as one having authority, and not in the manner of the scribes and the Pharisees. In our day, though, we often confuse speaking with *authority* with speaking as an *authoritarian*. We all experience the dogmatic, know-it-all person who pounds us over the head whether he is selling a refrigerator or religion. Most of us react negatively to the authoritarian person who limits our freedom to say no or who tries to manipulate us into doing something that either we don't want to do or are not sure about.

A neighbor may spend a month in Colorado, come back, enter our house and say, "John, we spent a wonderful two weeks at Estes Park. You should try it some time. It will change your life and give you a great period of relaxation."

18

That is considerably different from a neighbor's renting you a cabin, bringing you a plane ticket, and coercing you to go to Colorado. The example may be farfetched, but the point is not. The testimony of a witness can be helpful and tremendously persuasive—even authoritative. But, manipulation, arm-twisting, and coercion smack of authoritarianism, and we wish to avoid them like the plague.

Another way of looking at persuasive communication is to consider the role of *advocacy*. While on the one hand there are many people in our day who are dogmatic and authoritarian, there are on the other hand many people who are timid about being advocates. They are fearful that they may be authoritarian, so they are hesitant to express anything positively. They seem to assume that in a democracy, decisions are arrived at by people with no opinions who somehow deliberatively make decisions. In some instances of problem-solving, we do arrive at conclusions in that way. In the main, however, a democracy is not made up of people with no opinions, but just the opposite. A democracy is made up of people with contending opinions.

The same is true for Christians. A postbaptized Christian is an advocate. He or she wears that label. One who does so has made a commitment, and though the commitment might be lukewarm, it nonetheless identifies who that person is. A persuaded Christian is one who wishes to witness, testify, speak, and communicate that message to others. One does not have to cajole, harrass, threaten, or intimidate in order to be anxious for others to hear and respond.

The most important aspect of the communication process is the message itself. We have already indicated how important

19

the spoken word is in human relationships—that it is the vehicle. We have indicated the significance of the witness doing the speaking. And, we have affirmed the need for a receiver from whom a response can be sought. As necessary as all of these things are, none of them is as important as the content of the speech to be made, or the gospel to be communicated, or the message to be proclaimed. Though the separation between *content* and *delivery* should never be made consciously, there is no doubt that the *what* is more important than the *how*.

Whether it is a politician laying out his platform, a doctor speaking to a medical society, a teacher explaining an intricate math problem, or a Christian talking about his faith, the important part of any of these speeches is the content of the speech itself.

While the purpose of this book is methodology and not theology, it would be well for the Christian to be reminded that the most crucial aspect of his or her speaking will be the message itself. What one calls that message is not so important; the content of it surely is. Whether stated as the gospel, the good news, the Christ-event, salvation, or some other term, the one who purports to *speak* the faith must *know* the faith. Christians might differ in their specific emphases, but the central core of the Christian message is the same for all Christians: Jesus Christ is Lord. This good news is centered around the event of God's revelation in Jesus Christ. It is known by us in faith through the life, teachings, death, and resurrection of Jesus. Whatever else one communicates as a Christian, these central faith-facts should inform the substance of our speeches.

The content of the gospel message is important, then, because we have a specific "Word" to communicate through our words. It is not just our own experience—important as that is. It is not just a witness—as important as that can be. Nor is it just our testimony, though that too can be of great importance. The gospel is a message of great content, and it needs to be known not only with our hearts but with our minds. God's Word to us is a meaningful word. Therefore, we have to understand it ourselves before we can communicate it to others; we need to understand it in order to speak about it articulately; and we need to grasp it before we can be persuasive once we do begin to speak. Whatever else the gospel is—and it is many things—it is at least the communication of an idea.

To say that the gospel has a specific content and is a meaningful message impels us not only to be convinced of our message but to know it so well that we can convince others. Careful preparation becomes the mandate of the Christian speaker. The gospel is too important to be entrusted to fuzzy heads. My witness may be important, but it is not the message. My testimony may lead another to the church or strengthen the fallen, but in itself it is not the gospel. My experience of God's revelation may persuade another to faith, but proclaiming the Word is much more. Witness, testimony, and experience are not substitutes for the gospel. They become meaningful as they are related to the gospel.

The speaker, then, seeks to have a meaningful grasp of the message before speaking it. But, just as it would be wrong to assume that the gospel is a "feeling" that is lacking in intellectual content, so it is an error to believe that the gospel

21

is just "head talk." Much more than simply rational ideas is being communicated when one speaks. Earlier we suggested that even your "Good morning" may involve much more than the words, and that a preacher may say something different from his words in his manner. And a politician may seem in his attitude to be at war with his speech. All of these seem to suggest that communication goes on at more than one level.

The communication that accompanies the words of a speech consists of emotions, feelings, gestures, facial expressions, and bodily action—all of which may support or detract from what is being spoken. In the case of the insincere politician or the angry preacher, we have seen how these emotional factors can detract from the message. On the other hand, emotions and feelings can lend support to the words being expressed. When a person says "I love you," for example, the look of compassion and tenderness that accompanies these words also says "I love you." The combination of the words with the emotional elements communicates on the highest possible level. And what is true for the personal "I love you" is also true for a speaker in front of the audience. If he speaks of the grace of God that accepts the forgiven sinner, his own attitude of acceptance creates an experience of communication that includes the meaning of grace as basic. At the same time, that meaning is also encompassed with the feelings and emotions of acceptance.

One more thing. We should not forget that communication seeks a response. The word does not fall into a bottomless pit. People hear and respond. When the speaker affirms the

What happens?

grace of God in a manner that reflects his or her acceptance of that "good news," then the listeners through God's grace are enabled to feel acceptance. Then the proclamation of the gospel has become an event. If I accept the fact that God has accepted me when I hear that good word from the mouth of another, then that has truly become an event of salvation. The speaker is not just talking *about* the gospel; the speaker has created the gospel. At that very moment salvation has come into being.

In summary: So far we have made several affirmations that are indispensable for Christian communication.

1. The basis of communication is oral speech. Word, language, and speech all combine to make ours a verbal world. Speech is a uniquely human function and forms the groundwork for all communion among human persons.

2. The Christian gospel has traditionally been entrusted to the sound of the human voice. The spoken word has been and continues to be the vehicle that carries the Christian message.

3. Communication of a message seeks a response. We communicate with one another to elicit a response. As Christians we are enjoined to be advocates who witness to our faith. We do so unavoidably by the fact of the label we wear. Consciously we do it through persuasion, not intimidation.

4. At the heart of the Christian gospel is a message. That message is a meaningful one. It speaks clearly now, as it did then. We are not in the first instance communicating a feeling or a mood or an experience; we are communicating an idea. Though the gospel is more than an idea, it is at least that. To

23

speak of it means that one understands the meaning clearly before proposing to communicate it to others.

5. We communicate with spoken words, but we communicate nonvocally too. We "speak" on more than one level. Our attitudes, emotions, and manner will all be speaking too, either to support or detract from our verbal utterance.

6. The persons who listen are indispensable parts of the communication process. Their hearing and response cannot be excluded from the speech itself. The total event of communication includes the speaker, the message, and those who hear and respond.

2

Look Who's Talking!
(The Communicator)

All of us remember the old saying, "What you are speaks so loudly that I can't hear what you are saying." Interestingly enough, that is not so different from what Aristotle said many, many years ago when he talked about the elements of persuasion that arise from the speaker as the speech is delivered.

The ancient Greek rhetorician believed that a speaker reveals certain personal traits to his audience that will affect the audience's response to what he has to say. In fact, he contended that what a speaker reveals about himself is the most important factor in persuading an audience. Though Aristotle was concerned with the message of a speech—its content and argument—he nevertheless saw quite correctly that the speaker standing before an audience reveals through his delivery, and through his or her person, certain traits that could affect the audience's response tremendously. Three elements make up this category of ethical persuasion, or *ethos*. They are competence, character, and goodwill.

Our concern is not with ancient rhetoric but with modern communication. Yet, many of these old principles—which, of course, have changed considerably through the years—are still valid in their emphases. Other ancient and modern communicators—unlike Aristotle—believed that the reputation of the speaker, both before and after a speech, affected the speech. Aristotle limited himself to the speech itself. Others talked about the importance of the "good man" as a speaker. And, of course, more to the point for us, Christians like Augustine "baptized" rhetorical principles for the church.

The important thing is to emphasize that the *who* is all tied up with the *what* and the *how* of communicating. The audience makes certain judgments about the person speaking. They may be wrong or unfair; nevertheless, they do hear the speech in the light of how they feel about the speaker. The wise speaker needs to know that his or her own person will affect the message. This does not mean that one should become something one is not. One cannot work at being sincere. A person can be aware of an audience's possible reactions, however, and work on improving his or her effectiveness through sound principles of communication. While there is nothing sacred about Aristotle's understanding of competence, character, and goodwill, those categories are useful in providing an outline for a discussion of the speaker's role in the speech-event.

First, *competence*. Whether an audience perceives competence in the speaker is not important *only* for their belief in the speaker. Achieving competence is basic for the speaker regardless of the audience's concern. One way of looking at this whole book is to see it as a way of attaining competence in communication. A competent speaker is obviously more effective. A person speaking should not spend time worrying about whether the audience thinks he or she is competent; competency should be the goal in itself.

26

LOOK WHO'S TALKING!

One does not have to have a Phi Beta Kappa key or a college degree to be a competent speaker. <u>Knowledge and wisdom are not the same.</u> My own father was one of the most intelligent men I have ever known, and he had only an eighth-grade education. <u>Discipline, hard work, and study can give a speaker the kind of competence that enables him or her to be effective.</u>

Specifically, though, some areas of competency can be highlighted. First, *preparation*. Any speaker can be well-prepared for a speech occasion. We have all suffered painfully through lay Sunday sermons, conference reports, or speeches at the Rotary Club, where the speaker obviously was not prepared and thus attempted to speak "off the cuff." <u>A good speaker will be adequately prepared.</u> We will see more specifically how this preparation evolves when it comes <u>to getting the idea formulated and building the speech.</u> At this point, though, it is enough to say that we need to allow ourselves enough time before the speech is to take place to be thoroughly prepared. Such an attitude will go a long way towards ensuring not only the audience's perception of competency but the speaker's competence in speaking skills.

<u>Competency will also deal with such matters as gathering data for the speech, building the speech, and delivering it.</u> All of these will be discussed in the following pages. But, competency will also be concerned with the way we deal with opposing positions and the way we handle our arguments or those of others. We need to be aware of the temptation to speak with authority in fields we know little about simply because we have the floor. A comedian may be funny, well known, and popular. Because of his reputation he may also

1
CS Lewis

speak on politics and get a hearing. We sometimes forget that competency in one field does not necessarily make for expertness in another. For example, the cult of popularity can fool us into thinking a film star should be taken as seriously when he speaks on foreign policy as when he speaks on film direction. The point is particularly appropriate for lay persons who wish to speak effectively about faith. An accountant, a housewife, a business executive, or a filling station owner needs to remember that stepping out of one's own field should not hinder the desire to be an effective communicator of the faith. It does suggest, however, that expertness, competency, and knowledgeability should be established in order to be an effective Christian communicator. The gospel is too serious to be spoken of off the top of the head, even under the guise of personal witness.

The second area relevant to speech competency is *authenticity,* or *integrity.* Though the word *character* is more often used here, there are two reasons for not doing so. For one thing, *character* is a word that can include everything pertaining to a speaker's persuasive inventory, including competence itself and goodwill. Two, *character* is often thought of too moralistically or too narrowly, thus reducing the applicability of the term to our own particular style of life. But, to say a person is *authentic* means that he or she "rings true," is in tune with himself or herself, and that what he or she states with the lips is congruent with what is on the inside. We often refer to a friend as genuine—a person of integrity.

Qualities such as these fortunately are being communicated by the person who is speaking. Honesty *is* the best policy not only in business dealings but in public speaking. "Phoniness'' is difficult to hide no matter how effective our ability to speak. Of course, audiences can be fooled—for a time. And, too, they will occasionally misread even the best of persons. In the long run, however, the person who has ''got it all together'' in his or her internal life will be the most effective in putting it all together externally.

For the Christian communicator, it is clear upon what foundation our platform personality rests. It is a commitment to the gospel, to the church, and to increasing the love of God and neighbor. Our lives, if we speak upon Christian themes, should be in tune with that basic commitment. If they are so in tune, then the basic harmony that makes up integrity or authenticity will be assured. Not all of our life-styles will need to be the same, however. Another Christian communicator—preacher or lay person—may have habits, tastes, or manners that will not be yours. However, if these are congruent with his basic commitment, he can still be a man of integrity for you.

The basic commitment as a Christian, then, should be thought of more theologically than moralistically, or psychologically. In the first instance we are the channel of the message; we are not the message itself. We do not have to be little gods. Nor do we need to think that all communicators are absolutely whole persons in the psychological sense. One does not need to be entirely psychologically healthy before getting to one's feet. In some ways, an entirely integrated person in the psychological sense might not be the best communicator. Being a Christian in our day may very well give us too much heartsickness to be healthy and glib about anything—let alone the gospel.

29

Also, it should be emphasized that not all our speaking will necessarily be thought of in terms of Christian speaking or preaching. Many times we will be making speeches about the church's program or reports of a conference or a presentation at a church school class or a talk at a local service club luncheon. <u>Still, for the Christian communicator, it is well to keep in mind the basic commitment to the church as the basis for one's communication and as the groundwork affecting one's own integrity on the platform—whether a pulpit or a banquet table.</u>

The third quality of the speaker's persuasive ability, *goodwill,* has to do with his or her attitude toward the audience. An angry preacher remembering the board's rejection of his pet project on last Wednesday evening may be communicating hostility from the pulpit on Sunday by the set of his jaw, the cold eyes, or his angry tone, even though his subject is ''The Joys of Being a Christian.'' The audience reads—rightly or wrongly—the speaker's attitude toward them by the emotions he radiates from the platform. Sometimes this is unfortunate, for a shy speaker may be timid in delivery and thus communicate lack of interest. Nevertheless, the effective speaker needs to be aware of how he or she is ''going over'' and work on strengthening poor communication qualities.

<u>Too often speakers ignore the audience they address.</u> We <u>become so concerned with our subject or our own selves in communicating that we ignore those who are to receive our thoughts.</u> But in reality, <u>those whose function it is to hear are part of the process of communication itself.</u> The task of communication is not complete until the receivers have

30

heard. The audience, the occasion, and the particular purpose are all part of the preparation. As we shall see later, understanding the audience affects not only the speech itself but the reception of the message being uttered. Whatever that reception might be, the basic affirmation now is that a speaker's concern for those sitting "out there" will determine their interest and response to what he is saying.

It seems clear, then, that these qualities of competence, integrity, and goodwill—basic to the speaker and viewed by the audience in the speech occasion—cannot be limited to the speech itself. What precedes a speech and what follows it are part and parcel of the speaker's speech. We are not isolated human beings cut off from others who from time to time make a speech. What we are as individuals—as friends, husbands, wives, fathers, sons—all goes to make up who we are as persons. That not only will be communicated as we speak; it is part of people's knowledge of us before we begin. The speech may be received well because of the positive feelings the audience have about us before they come to hear us. On the other hand, the speech may not be received well because of previous negative feelings the audience might have had.

The speech may, of course, change the audience's mind either negatively or positively. And, we cannot change in order to be more acceptable to an audience. The important idea is to be aware that our speech is tied in with who we are, that it begins before we speak, and continues after we finish. For the Christian communicator, the point is evident. Our commitment is not limited to the speech occasion. Our Christian commitment before and after the speech is part of the one we make before the audience. And, what we communicate in the speech is inseparable from the way we are perceived before and after the speech takes place.

For the Christian communicator, the impact of the who on the speech is obvious. We have already seen that historically the Christian has a precedent for believing that speaking in God's name is an important aspect of the good news that God brings to mankind. On a less lofty note, the speaker on a religious theme is filtering that idea through his or her person. Phillips Brooks, speaking of preaching, once said that "preaching is bringing of truth through personality." Whether preaching or lay speaking, the person doing the talking is integrally related to the message being brought.

Sometimes we are concerned so much about the burden we carry in being a Christian communicator that we do not wish to do it at all. Or, we may feel we are not worthy enough to be a bearer of God's word. Or, we may be too tense and filled with stage fright to be an effective speaker. All of these feelings are understandable, and they are apt to plague all speakers on some occasions. The experienced speaker or the novice each face these anxieties. They are not new or novel. They can be explained and handled. They need not handicap anyone from being effective on his or her feet.

The idea that we speak for God or that we are God's messengers and conveyers of the Word to others should not paralyze us. For one thing, ours is an incarnational faith. God entered history as a man. And he still does. To affirm that means to affirm that our humanity is accepted by God. Paul could refer to himself as the least of the saints. God chose what is weak in the world to shame the strong. We are not

32

asked to be gods; we are asked to be human. No one can cry, "I'm not good enough to speak for God." God chooses that his word be carried by human beings. That should be enough for any of us.

In addition, God is the center of our message; we are not. Taken seriously, that is a comforting thought. We are to share Christ's love, but we do not need to be a "little Jesus." We are not a model who might easily confuse people into believing that they must mimic us. We are channels for the gospel—not the gospel itself. Too often Christian speakers have felt that they must "save" others or be the persons upon whom the salvation of others depends. It is true that we can be the channels of God's grace, but it is God who saves people. We minister as Christians in his name, but we are not Jesus. Seeing our role clearly helps us understand that we are not the focus of our speaking. We point to another. Such a stance can relieve us of some of our anxiety.

More than that, it is also important to realize that so-called stage fright is not an altogether bad thing. One who speaks on a serious religious theme should not be alarmed to discover that there are some anxious feelings about delivering a speech. A speaker who affirms that he or she never feels nervous may be saying little to be nervous about. A speaker who senses the religious theme as a matter of life and death will undoubtedly be concerned when he or she stands before people. However, to feel that way need not paralyze one. Instead, it can give one the impetus to be effective when the moment comes to deliver the speech.

Even when not speaking on a Christian theme, some

newcomers to speaking will still be fearful about the speech situation. That, too, is natural. We all know how adrenalin flowing into the bloodstream heightens one's tension but also peaks one's abilities. Whether it is a soldier under fire, a football player before a big game, a lawyer trying a difficult case, or a person speaking before a group, there is something about the experience that brings nervousness, but also heightened awareness. As long as the tension is channeled constructively, it causes no alarm. It is only a problem when it paralyzes.

Overcoming stage fright can be managed in several different ways. First, as we have mentioned, we should recognize that it is quite normal, and accept it as such. Second, to minimize fear we should increase our preparation. Much of the material in this book focuses on how to get ready for and deliver a speech. At this point it can be said that the fear quotient can be diminished as the preparation quotient rises. A good idea, soundly grasped and prepared well, goes a long way towards dispelling the clouds of fear. Third, gaining confidence through practice and experience will enable one to speak well even if the butterflies do come.

The speaker, then, will be conscious of the seriousness of his or her purpose. Even though the speech situation may bring anxiety, it can be an exciting and challenging experience. The speaker who accepts tension can also triumph over it. Effective preparation and delivery of the speech is the answer.

In summary: The speaker's role in the delivery of the speech has several emphases:

LOOK WHO'S TALKING!

1. The speaker himself or herself may be more important *discuss* persuasively than anything he or she says about the subject. The who is being communicated as well as the what.

2. A speaker's personal persuasion grows out of competence, integrity, and goodwill. The audience will detect these from the speech. The speaker will consider them indispensable to his or her makeup as a person as well as a speaker.

3. What we are as persons before and after a speech is vitally related to the speeches we give. We cannot separate our total lives from the speech situation.

4. So-called stage fright can be controlled by the speaker, not vice versa. Tension before speaking is normal because of the seriousness of the speech and the unfamiliarity of the place and occasion. Preparation, though, can reduce tension to a manageable feeling of excitement.

3

Is Anybody Listening?
(Audience)

Sören Kierkegaard said that most people go to church the way they attend the theater. The preacher is the actor, and they are the critics who praise or blame, as the case may be. In reality, says Kierkegaard, the audience is on the stage, the preacher is the prompter who is whispering the lines they should be uttering, and God is the Critic-Judge—the real audience. Whether that analogy is altogether true or not, there is a sense in which any audience should be "on the stage" as far as the speaker's concern for them.

Unfortunately, most of us as speakers are so concerned with the speech we are to give that we do not devote much time to analyzing the audience who will hear us talk. Such self-concern is understandable. We are talking about serious matters in our religious themes, the content of what we say is vitally important, and the responsibility we have to be well prepared weighs heavily on our hearts and minds. None of these concerns, however, should blind us to the fact that those who will hear us also need a great deal of attention in the building of the speech.

Though there are many ways such an analysis could be approached, it might be helpful to isolate three general areas that need specific attention before the speech is given: the purpose of the speech, the setting or occasion, and the response sought. The speaker who takes these specific areas seriously can avoid unexpected pitfalls and, more importantly, can insure the chance for success in the speech situation.

First, what is the purpose of the speech? Often we assume the purpose. For example, if we are speaking to a church congregation, we may assume that the purpose is clear: they are all Christians, they are there to worship, they are all eager believers, they are all interested in what will be said, and so on. All of these assumptions may be wrong—even in the context of the religious setting. Even the minister with a rather homogeneous and predictable congregation will need to ask the purpose of his sermon from week to week; for the purpose may vary and the response of the congregation may be quite different. For example, next Sunday may be Budget Sunday. How would that affect the sermon knowing that the purpose is to raise funds? Next Sunday the message may be attuned to betterment of race relations, since it is Brotherhood Sunday. The purpose or the occasion may condition the speech in its preparation and its delivery.

What is true for the preacher is true for the rest of us. We all need to understand thoroughly the purpose of the speech as part of our preparation. Many times the purpose is conditioned by the invitation to speak. For example, our church may ask us to speak for five minutes during the worship service on ''What the Church Means to Me.'' Or we may be asked to speak on Budget Sunday about finance. Possibly we may be called to make a report to a board meeting on a conference we have attended as a representative

37

of the church. In these cases, the purpose is clear from the invitations and the topics assigned.

However, many times we will be on our own. The invitation may be so general that we are left to formulate our own topic. A service club may ask us to speak at lunch; the minister may ask us to pinch-hit some Sunday; we may be asked to lead a retreat for lay persons; or we may be invited to teach an adult Sunday school class. While in some general ways there may be an implied purpose, the specific purpose of the speech is in our hands, and we should formulate that clearly. For that reason, it is very helpful if, in addition to enunciating a thesis for the speech, the speaker is urged to develop a specific purpose—in writing—and affix it to the study outline along with the thesis. These two items will give unity and clarity to the speech.

Closely related to the purpose of the speech is the occasion or setting of the event to which we have been asked. Some analysis should be done in regard to several situational factors. Above we have considered the purpose, which deals with similar analysis, but we can be even more specific. What is the actual occasion? A youth retreat? A prayer breakfast? A church congregation? Any of these might condition our speech differently. A youth retreat might be outdoors, with everyone informally dressed and no lectern or podium on which to place notes. The prayer breakfast may be in a basement dining room around tables, with the speech given in the context of banging pots and pans or while members of the audience are leaving to get to work. Or, suppose we are in an auditorium with the group scattered in the back and fifteen or twenty rows vacant between the speaker's stand and the audience. Do we ask the audience to move to the front? Would we risk leaving the platform and going down into the midst of the audience? Any one of these situations could cause problems, not only for the novice, but for the experienced speaker as well. That is why we should try to discover everything we can about a speech situation before it occurs. Each speech-event should be "scouted" before the delivery, and this scouting should be considered a part of the preparation. Even the apparently "normal" congregation can add factors that must be contemplated before the actual occasion, such as the order of worship and the time allotted for the speech.

A factor such as timing may be more important than we think. Suppose we have prepared a twenty-minute talk, but after we get to the building, our host says that we only have ten minutes. Or, worse still, suppose we already know we have only fifteen minutes, but talk thirty. Both examples can cause a crisis. In the former, we have not had enough prior information. In the latter, our own lax preparation may cost us the attention and interest of the crowd while diminishing the chances for a favorable response and destroying our credibility and ethos. The length of the speech should be ascertained before the occasion, and the speech should be prepared with a specific time limit in mind—even if it involves practicing.

There are many other factors to be considered as well. One, for example, is the size of the crowd. As much as possible, that should be considered during the preparation period of the speech. Why? Suppose one is speaking to a small group of church leaders at a retreat. The setting may be informal, the crowd limited to fifteen or twenty and everyone seated. Such a situation would condition the speech given. Chances are the speaker would be seated too, notes would be out of place, the speech would be informal, and the delivery extremely conversational. Compare that with the typical Sunday service, and one can see the difference the setting, occasion, purpose, and crowd size would make. In the latter, there would be more people, a more formal setting, a different purpose for the speech, and a different delivery necessary in order to communicate effectively with those assembled.

Even age makes a difference. A speech to a junior-high group at church, the senior class in the local high school, or the retirement home will present varied challenges for the speaker. The first group would condition the speech toward simplicity of language, the need for arresting and dramatic material, and a delivery that would command attention. A local high-school assembly would condition choice of subject matter and suggest potential problems with holding attention, finding a common ground with the students, and seeking suitable challenges to command respect and interest. The retirement group would need comfort, hope, strength, and faith. These instances are intended simply to show the complexities of preparing a speech. Each occasion suggests its own special treatment to the conscientious speaker.

The third and possibly most important of the considerations concerning the audience is the response that is sought. What does the speaker want the audience to do about what is being said, if anything? The desired response should be thought through carefully and then enunciated in the study as part of the preparation of the speech. In short, the speaker could have on his basic outline a thesis, a brief word on the purpose of the speech and its setting or occasion, and a specifically worded "response sought."

The thesis of the speech answers the question What am I saying? The purpose states Why am I saying it? The occasion could refer to Where am I saying it? and the response sought says What do I want done about it? Another cryptic way of stating the response would be to answer the important question So what? Wording a response, like a thesis and a well-defined purpose, gives unity to be sure; but it gives a direction and a goal as well. Further, even one's delivery is affected by the response one is seeking.

Let's look at some examples of seeking a response. Suppose as a láy person you have been asked to speak at a Sunday morning service on Budget Sunday about the importance of giving to the church. Maybe an "Every Member Canvass" is to follow, or a pledge drive, or a plea for tithes. You are given five minutes to speak. It is conceivable, and even probable, that though the focus of the speech would be on the reasons for supporting the church, the conclusion might point directly to turning in pledge cards at the end of the service. If so, that specific response sought would condition the nature of the speech both as to content and delivery. In the former, it would give a goal and direction to which the content would point. In the latter, consciously or not, the delivery would have undoubtedly more urgency, since the response sought demands some specific action.

In another case, making a report to a board meeting about a conference one attended as a representative of the church would be completely different. The content of the report, though still having a thesis and outline, would be in the mode of summary, narrative, and insights gained. The response would perhaps be something diffuse and general; for example, "I want you to share my interest" or "You can be a better church member through these things I learned." The response, as in any speech, would be important for the speaker to think through before he or she delivers the speech. It does not matter whether a specific response is sought or not.

Part of the preplanning that goes into the assessment of the audience before projecting the response to the speech takes into consideration areas other than the ones mentioned thus far. For example, although it is difficult to generalize about audiences as a whole, it is possible to discern certain characteristics that should be taken into account by the speaker before the speech-event occurs. We have already mentioned that setting, size, and age have an effect; and there are other factors similar to age that can be probed if one is not too hasty with generalizations.

A rural community would have certain common interests that would, in turn, affect their general outlook on life and society. Their closeness to nature, the rhythm of seedtime and harvest, their views on farm supports, and the organizations to which they belong would condition their thinking. These would affect the speaker's perception of their response to his subject. It would also affect his vocabulary, illustrations, and content. On the other hand, though, it would be wrong to conclude that *rural* meant "unenlightened," "narrow," or "isolated." With good roads, college possibilities, and television, the so-called rural areas of America are as up-to-date as large cities, and their citizens are as well informed.

Another community might be a blue-collar section of a large city near a huge factory. Many of these people would be employed by the same company and belong to the same unions. They might find similar recreational outlets and even be of the same national origins. Their perceptions might very well be similar, their voting habits mostly the same, and their predispositions and mind-sets predictable. Other communities could be delineated as well. The small, county-seat town, the college community, the ethnic minority section of a ghetto, an upper-class suburb, all have distinctive characteristics that are clues to understanding their situation. Further, such insight is essential for the wise speaker who wishes to communicate with such a group, let alone seek a specific response from them.

It should be stated quickly that this knowledge of an audience's predisposition is not sought in order to manipulate them. We are not talking about the Christian speaker in terms of the high-pressure huckster who is probing an audience's background in order to play to their prejudices. There have been politicians who foment racial hatred by playing on the fears of those who live in the suburbs near the large cities. Our concern is with the religious communicator who has high ideals, stands in the context of a gospel of good news, and is ethically oriented. And, thus, his purpose is different. First of all, his concern is communication. Unless a speaker knows where an audience is, he cannot communicate with them. It is as simple as that. After that basic communication is established, the seeking of a response will depend upon knowing an audience's general mind-set and predisposition. However, there will be nothing hidden about that. The response sought can be open and above board, and the audience should have the freedom to say no as well as yes.

An audience will not only have certain general characteristics that identify it as a unit, but it will also have individual characteristics that might be called needs. Without getting into the murky waters of psychology, any good speaker will want to be aware of the drives that most of us have that motivate action. Here again, we need to know them not only in order to motivate them to some specific response, but to communicate on the most basic level. Persuasion is not manipulative; propaganda is.

What are some of these basic needs or drives that humans have? Certainly one of the most basic has to do with our desire for self-esteem. Some might call this pride, the tendency to think well of ourselves, or ego-strength. Theologians have called this need original sin, considering this drive a basic predisposition to deifying self instead of God. All of us are aware of the battle that goes on within all of us to appreciate who we are as God's children—a little lower than the angels—over against the perennial cry of the apostle Paul, that the good that he would do he did not, and the evil that he would refrain from he did. To love one's neighbor as oneself does not mean to love neighbor and not self; it means to keep that balance between appreciation of the human person under God and the will toward self that tends to place our own interests over those of others.

The speaker—whatever his audience—needs to recognize

44

this drive within his or her own self of course; but certainly he must apply this recognition to his audience as well. In the religious setting this ambivalent need can be graphically dramatized. There are many persons who are so guilt-ridden and sin-possessed that they do not believe God can forgive them. They think so little of themselves because of some sin they committed long ago that they believe God has never blotted the sin out and accepted them just the same. On the other hand, there are some people who think so highly of themselves that they have never understood the pervasiveness of sin—how we twist our own natures to put ourselves in the best light and others in lesser estimation. They have trouble making a true prayer of confession because they don't really believe they are that bad, certainly not "miserable offenders."

discuss

The able speaker will need to be sensitive to this precarious balance that resides in all persons. To the first group who are possessed by guilt and burdened by self-hate, the gospel of good news needs to be spoken affirmatively. A person does not need to be scolded; rather, he needs to be reminded that God does forgive, does accept, and does blot out past mistakes. The persons who think more highly of themselves than they ought to, who thank God that they are not like others, need to be reminded of the peril of pride, the sin of idolatry, and the risk of placing self over God.

Love for others is one of our basic drives too. Sometimes this need is thought of as the sexual drive or the desire to reproduce. However, that is too narrow a view and is too often thought of in simply sexual terms. Love certainly can involve the love for a mate, sexual and otherwise. It also

45

comprises affection, admiration, friendship, and concern for others. Christians have no problem understanding the nature of love as Paul expressed it in I Corinthians 13. This love for others is particularly strong in religious people, and the speaker who is talking about the mission program of the church will understand an audience's positive reactions when the appeal is made on the Christian basis of love for neighbor—remembering that neighbor is not limited by geography.

Altruism is close to if not part of love itself. It is the desire to do things for others. Certainly religious people have this in strong degree. Most of us do—whatever our religious or nonreligious label. The soldier who adopts an orphan in the middle of a war, the service club members who volunteer for work with the handicapped, the office staff who solicit for the United Fund, or the housewives who serve as hospital aides—all are motivated in part by altruistic motives. Picture a speaker in front of any one of the above groups trying to get support for his or her cause and it is easy to see the appeal that should be at the heart of the speech.

There are undoubtedly many other desires within human nature that call for careful consideration by the speaker. I have singled out these three basic ones to illustrate the need of the speaker to be aware of any forces within the individuals of an audience that need to be tapped in order to motivate them persuasively. Indeed, one must be aware of them even to communicate effectively.

In summary: The wise speaker should consider the audience with the same seriousness that he or she would consider the subject. To make an objective analysis of the audience, several factors should be kept in mind.

1. The speaker should clarify the purpose of the speech to be given. Even though the purpose may seem obvious by the invitation, the familiarity with the audience, or the context of the speech, the thoughtful speaker will formulate the specific purpose before the speech occasion.

2. Each speech occasion needs specific analysis. Such factors as the location, the setting, time allotted, size of the crowd, and the predominant age group are examples of factors that should be taken into consideration in preparing the speech.

3. Each speech needs a clearly worded "response sought." Whether it is a speech of information or one that seeks to motivate the audience to some specific action, the speaker should consciously think through the desired response.

4. Audiences have certain general characteristics that affect their responses to a given speaker, speech, and subject. The well-prepared speaker makes an analysis of these characteristics in planning the speech.

5. As individuals, we all have certain needs, drives, and desires. A persuasive speaker is one who knows these needs and adapts to them. The concern is not to "manipulate" or coerce; it is, first of all, to communicate, then, to "motivate."

4

What's the Big Idea?
(Sources for the Speech)

There is an old story in which a man tells how to make rabbit pie. "You makes your dough, mixes the makin's, cooks it in the oven till it's brown, but not too brown—but first you catches your rabbit." There's no rabbit pie without the rabbit; there is no speech without an idea.

We have already suggested that for the Christian communicator the gospel itself is the heart of the message. The content of the faith will be the backdrop for speeches made in pulpit or on platform within the general context of Christian groups. However, we need to be much more specific in building a speech than saying that it is generally Christian. Further, some of our speaking may not necessarily be *religious* in the usual sense of that term. But the basic principles of communication will be valid in any speech situation.

Figuratively speaking, Christian communicators stand in and between two worlds. On the one side, there is their commitment to the Christian gospel and all that that means. On the other, there is the secular world in which we all live. This is not to say that the division between the secular and the sacred is rigid, nor that the worlds we are describing do not overlap. Simply speaking, the analogy suggests only that the ideas for speeches can come from either dimension of a person's experiences.

On the one side, there is the gospel of good news. That would include our Christian experience, the church, the Bible, our theology, our personal commitment, and our life-styles. The Christian commitment would be the philosophy that undergirds all areas in which we live, move, and have our being. The other side concerns our workaday world. Here would be our secular vocations, the world of events that surround us, the human beings who cross our paths, the news, television, music, drama, and all the psychological and sociological expressions of human beings in their various relationships. A speech on a religious theme could have its inception in either plane.

For example, one might be reading the Bible devotionally and be intrigued once again by the story of the prodigal son—perhaps because one sees oneself in one of the characters in a way not seen before. Maybe instead of focusing on the prodigal son, as is often done, one sees with clear eyes the role of the elder brother and decides that that is where too many Christians stand. From that base, the speech could develop around the temptation of Christians to look down their noses at those who have lived wasted lives—even if they repent—and fail to see the unforgiving spirits, the selfishness, and the pride that resides in those who feel they are the ''good'' Christians and have never lived in the ''pigpens'' of the world.

Or, the speech could go the other way. We may be reminded in Lent of the emphasis that Christians place upon sacrifice—at least symbolically. But instead of thinking of giving up cigarettes or chewing gum, we attempt to go deeper in our faith; and that leads to an examination of Abraham's sacrifice of Isaac. In both the cases cited, the speeches would be founded upon the Bible. In one, the idea begins with the Bible and leads to the secular implications. In the other, the idea begins with a specific theme and develops by reference to the biblical story.

The important point to remember here is that there must be a basic idea before there can be a speech at all—let alone a speech on an important religious theme. Some of us seem to have a good many ideas. They come to us easily from all parts of our life, we burst at the seams with themes that clamor for expression. Others of us scratch our heads to find ideas, stumble over ideas everyday that could be fruitful if we only had eyes to see, and get "uptight" when we are faced with a chance to speak but cannot think of anything to talk about. In either case, the effective speaker develops a method for gathering materials, preserving ideas, and maintaining "grist for the mill."

Though no one method will serve for everyone, there are some steps that are helpful to all of us who wish to be effective communicators. First of all, the broader one's interests, the better the specific speaker one is. Though there is a danger, of course, that a person could be wide and not deep, there is a greater problem in being too narrow. John Wesley said that the world was his parish. A good speaker might observe that the world is his parish also, when it comes to finding ideas. Just as a bush in the desert became a flaming torch for Moses, so can the ordinary events become exciting

50

ways of opening up ideas for proclaiming the Christian message.

Therefore, the first thing the effective speaker needs to remember is that he or she is gathering materials from a broad realm of life experiences. We need to be aware of the breadth of our interests, and to be sensitized to a wide scope of life that does not necessarily carry the label "religious." "This is our Father's world" not only in music but also in the search for ideas. We have already seen how the ethos of a speaker is important; so basically we assume that the would-be or experienced speaker is sensitive to people, likes them, and has broad sympathies for humanity at large. Assuming that this is true—and if it is not the speaker may fail no matter how good the materials in the speech—then we can think specifically of getting materials together for a speech.

For many of us, the best way to widen our horizons is through reading. This would include reading the Bible, of course, but it also suggests reading in so-called secular areas as well. And, it is reading with a purpose. While no one would want to read only to look for an idea that is usable in a speech for next Sunday night, it is nevertheless true that the alert speaker will seldom read anything unless he or she has in mind the possibility that something will jump off the page and suggest its usefulness for a speech some day. Though each of us differs as persons, and therefore in our tastes, some general suggestions might be helpful in directing our reading.

Apart from the Bible (which we will discuss in more detail later in the chapter) and religious papers and magazines, we should keep abreast of the happenings in the world. Aside from our local, daily, or weekly papers and television, one could very well determine to read carefully a weekly news magazine like *Newsweek* or *Time*. Such reading keeps one up-to-date on the national and world news, as well as special features such as movies, plays, books, and religion. In addition, some might find it helpful to read outstanding papers like *The New York Times* and *The Christian Science Monitor*, to get the larger national perspective. Other magazines come to mind. One of my favorites through the years has been the *Saturday Review*. Others will have preferences for *Harper's, Atlantic Monthly,* and so on. The specific selections are not as important as the fact that the speaker is consciously developing a systematic reading program. The United Methodist Church has many publications that come to one's home or church regularly. Reading such magazines as *The Interpreter,* the *New World Outlook,* or *engage/social action* will keep the lay speaker abreast of the news of the church in the world and at the same time provide ideas suitable for his speaking needs.

As important as reading is, though, it will not be helpful to speakers unless some effort is made to preserve the ideas picked up in the reading. Of course, reading is good for its own sake—it develops the person. A well-rounded person has good ethos as a communicator. But, more specifically, the communicator is a craftsman and must give attention to honing the tools in preparation for building the speech. This means, among other things, that each person must find some methodology for reading, taking notes, and keeping the materials ready and available for use when needed. Though each person will differ in methods—as one differs from another in talents—some suggestions may nevertheless be helpful to all, whatever the stage of development as a speaker.

Above all, we must make some conscious commitment to preserving our insights. All of us have had the experience of reading something that sparked our interest, forgetting to write it down, and hours later finding it has evaporated. Or, we have thought of an exciting idea at night, and by morning it has disappeared. A conscious attention to intentional reading will help us avoid losing our most interesting insights. Several ways are open to us for capturing ideas for future use.

If we are reading a book that is our own, one effective procedure is to underline key passages. Then, at the end of the book a list of page numbers with tentative topics can be listed for future reference. There are many ways in which these underlined materials can be used. Later they can be copied on cards, with an appropriate topic on each, and filed in alphabetical order. Or, they may be transferred to a journal or notebook, either by copying the passages one wishes to preserve or by simply noting the topics or subject heads one has listed at the end of the book. The form used is not important; the fact of keeping material available and accessible is of tremendous importance.

Similar to this procedure is the necessity of reading newspapers and magazines with an eye for valuable subject material. A pair of scissors is a good tool to have at one's side. It is best to clip out the items that attract your attention right away. Give them a subject head, and file them in manila folders or in one large folder, keeping the items current by checking through the folder regularly as you prepare speeches.

When reading books that belong to others, such as library books, a speaker should keep file cards, paper, or a notebook nearby to copy down useful quotations, to record significant passages, to jot down page references for rereading, and to write down the ideas that form as a result of the reading. These ideas are some of the most valuable results of your reading. They belong to you and will have their impact on future speeches—but they must first be recorded.

I have been specific with my suggestions for reading, taking notes, and recording ideas but there are many other methods; and each person needs to find his or her own style. File systems can be simple or elaborate. There are a hundred different ways of preserving materials for future use. The method is not important. What cannot be overemphasized is that some systematic method of capturing and keeping ideas gleaned from reading is a must for a speaker. And not only reading. Ideas gathered from observing people, listening to the radio while driving, or even watching movies also may prove worth keeping. A small pocket notebook or a small cassette tape recorder kept by one's side in the car or by the bedstand at night may be the means of capturing a fresh insight that otherwise might be lost.

Earlier we suggested that we would discuss the use of the Bible in some detail. Much of what was said above would be appropriate to Bible study as well; for we need to read the Bible in terms of the ideas that possess us, as well as for devotional reading. But, the Bible needs to be given a special treatment; for the religious speaker should be a person of *one*

54

book, even as John Wesley spoke of himself. One does not need to be a sophisticated scholar of the Bible, but we are all called to be faithful students of God's Word. As Christians and as Christian speakers, we are compelled to study the book that records God's revelation to us through the community of faith—the church.

In the first chapter, the nature of the gospel was alluded to, and that Word comes to us through the Scriptures. Our concern here is not specifically theological; it is methodological. The faithful Christian will read the Bible. The Christian speaker (as the clergy) will study the Bible in order to be a faithful expositor of the Word found there. Here again, methods will vary.

There are many ways to read and study the Bible. One may include Bible reading as part of the daily devotional period. Or, one may study the Bible systematically, reading it book by book or perhaps following a lectionary, a selection of scripture readings organized around the Church Year. Most churches have such a selection of lessons and even the "free" churches follow the Church Year—however loosely—and read appropriate lessons.

Following a plan of study such as the one provided by a lectionary has much to recommend it. For one thing, it assures the speaker of exposure to a broad range of scripture, not just his or her favorite passages. Also, such a program of selected scripture gives the listeners an opportunity to hear the Bible opened up to them, and permits the speaker to have a planned program of study for his own development. Finally, and most importantly, it gives the speaker a source of new, fresh, and important ideas from the Bible without his having to first of all "think up" themes and then try to find verses in the Bible to support or proof-text the ideas.

Let us begin by sitting down with our Bibles. Whether following a specific series of lessons for study, reading devotionally as meditation, or reading at random, it is well to read with notebook in hand. Ideas that leap up from the pages, God's Word that speaks, insights that one has—all need to be recorded as they occur.

Though there are a host of ways in which a biblical sermon or speech can be constructed, it may be helpful to single out a few of them. Let's imagine ourselves with a specific passage in front of us. How do we get hold of the meaning so that we can interpret it to others? Obviously, we have to understand what that passage is saying before we can say what it means. One good way to do this is to read it over several times, permitting the words to "speak" to us as we read. Ideas that leap out of the scripture should be written down. These are first impressions, tentative ideas, and even "feelings" about what the scripture is saying. Later they may need to be changed, but in the early stages, ideas that come should be put on paper.

A next step would be to compare this passage with its other translations. Those of us who cannot use the original languages of Greek and Hebrew need not be handicapped. One of the best ways to proceed is to remember that we are not limited to only one version of the Bible. Read the scripture in all of the versions you have in your study, and, of course, there should be several. Looking at the verses in several different translations will give shading of meanings that will bring clarity as well as variety to the material.

Then, one should begin a serious study of the passage in order to find out specifically what the meaning is. To do this, he or she should utilize the tools at his or her disposal. Lay persons—speakers or not—need commentaries to help them unlock the meaning of the Bible. Such books as *The Interpreter's Bible, The Interpreter's Dictionary of the Bible,* or *The Interpreter's One-Volume Commentary on the Bible* are the kinds of help needed to study the Bible with seriousness. In addition, there are volumes such as *Proclamation: Aids for Interpreting the Lessons of the Church Year,* a series of paperbacks that treats passages both as to their meaning and their interpretation. There are word-study books on the Bible that are also helpful. A visit to a religious bookstore will turn up a number of good aids for Bible study. A concordance, for example, would be of great value; for it shows how different themes can be found in various parts of the Scriptures. Many Bible versions will have notes in the margins and references to other places in the Bible where a theme reoccurs.

Suppose we have before us the twelfth chapter of Paul's letter to the Romans. We have read it in several versions: the Revised Standard, the King James, the New English Bible, Jerusalem Bible, and others. Perhaps we have jotted down some ideas that have come to us. When we come to the serious work of study, we may need first of all to ask about words we don't understand. For example, what did Paul mean by the word "sacrificed" in verse 1? or, by the phrase "heap burning coals" in verse 20?

We need, then, to look at key words or even key sentences that may not be clear at first reading. The word-study books or commentaries will help us here. We also need to know something about the Bible book itself, about the author (in this case, Paul), and about the situation in which the writing occurs. (Why was Paul in jail? To whom was he writing specifically?) What are the main themes of the book? What issues are raised in this passage? How do they relate to the biblical viewpoint or to the Christian gospel as a whole? What is the theological meaning? What is the truth here that the church affirms? How does this passage relate to the gospel proclamation? Questions like these are not farfetched but should be asked and dealt with as one does one's study of the biblical record. The commentaries help us to understand.

After taking these steps, we can begin to ask what is the "spiritual" meaning of the passage? What does it say to us, in other words, what is God trying to say to us through this passage? It is after this kind of difficult but rewarding work that the speaker begins to ask the question, What does this important chapter say to the church, or to my people, or to my day, life, and time? When the Bible has been approached with this seriousness, then the speaker has truly done the kind of study that prepares him or her to speak earnestly to others about the gospel of Jesus Christ. The central idea for a particular talk will evolve from such study, and the speaker will begin to build the speech from the meaning it offers.

Whether Bible study is intended for a specific speech or for general research, the resulting ideas should be written down and filed away the same as those from secular sources.

In summary, getting the idea for a speech involves certain important steps.

WHAT'S THE BIG IDEA?

1. Speech ideas—even for religious speeches—come from both secular and "sacred" sources. Even though those two worlds overlap, we can gather materials specifically from the secular world in which we live or from the world of faith that contains the church.

2. Some (or much) of our speaking will not be in the realm of proclaiming the faith. We may be called upon to teach Sunday school classes, present reports, talk about a conference, address a men's group, or lead a prayer breakfast. Whether proclaiming the gospel or talking within the context of the church's work, the principles for gathering and presenting data are largely the same.

3. Every speech should have at its heart a central idea. Though that seems obvious, many speeches fail here. They may have too many ideas or several fuzzy ideas. An effective talk has one—and only one—clear idea.

4. A speaker should read widely in order to broaden his or her interests, sensitize his or her nature, and gather ideas for speaking. This reading should be wide in scope, and though inclusive of Bible and devotional reading, it should not be limited to that.

5. The ideas gathered in reading should be preserved by taking notes and keeping files, journals, or notebooks. The methods of doing so are not important, but the necessity is there.

6. The Bible is the basic source of our speaking, and serious study of the Scriptures is indispensable to it.

5

Hey!
Look Where You're Going!
(Organizing the Idea)

It has been reported in several places that a minister whose father was also a preacher received some very interesting advice from the older man. The son was asked to send his father a night lettergram every Saturday, summarizing the message of his Sunday sermon. Not only was this a way for the father to keep up with the son, it was a way to teach the young minister the importance of clarity and conciseness. My own judgment is that a twenty-five-word night letter is too long. A one-sentence day wire would be better, and even then the sentence should be short.

The basic step in refining the idea for a speech is to formulate a *thesis*. The difference between an idea and a thesis is simple, but the distinction is important. The idea is a general subject about which one is speaking. The thesis is specifically what one is saying about the theme, subject, or idea. The thesis is similar to a proposition in a debate. It is a one-sentence statement of what you intend to say in the speech you are to make. The one-sentence wire alluded to above would be a thesis. The basic idea of a passage like Genesis 11:1-9, which is the story of the Tower of Babel, may very well be idolatry. "Come, let us build ourselves a city, and a tower with its top in the heavens, and let us make a name for ourselves." God's answer to that was to confuse the language of an entire people and to scatter them abroad. The *thesis* of a speech on that passage would be the speaker's reaction to the idea of idolatry it portrays. A one-sentence statement such as, "Our attempt to be gods always ends in failure" would be a thesis. Different theses could be formulated depending on what is to be said in the speech and what direction it is to take.

The importance of a clear thesis cannot be over-emphasized. Whether one is giving a meditation, a sermon, a talk to lay persons about the budget, or a Christmas message to a Rotary Club, the essential item in the presentation is a clearly enunciated thesis. With all due apologies to Paul, "Though I speak with the tongues of men and of angels, and have not *clarity,* I am as sounding brass or a tinkling cymbal." A member of a congregation made a biting comment about the sermon he was listening to one Sunday morning. He said that the preacher was ten minutes into the sermon, and he, the listener, did not have the foggiest notion of what the minister was talking about other than that he was on the side of religion. Whether a sermon, a talk before the PTA, or a witness at a prayer breakfast, most speeches fail as far as content is concerned because they are not clear.

Why is clarity in speaking so important? The answer is simple. Whether preaching, witnessing, testifying, or in any way communicating the Christian gospel to others, we are basically communicating an idea. The Christian message is certainly more than an idea, a thought, a rational proposition, or a mental concept. A speaker will be communicating more than ideas and words. There will be feelings, emotions, spirit, mood, and many other nonverbal aspects of communication. But, at the center, there is a meaningful idea. The Christian gospel makes sense. And, in order to communicate that meaningful idea, the speaker must have it clearly in his mind and be able to articulate it clearly for his listeners. Thus the importance of undergirding our speeches with a clear thesis cannot be overemphasized.

The thesis should be reducible to one sentence. If it cannot be, the speaker is probably trying to cover too much in the speech. In fact, even a long, involved complex or compound sentence suggests that the speech will have too much in it or that the central idea is not clear enough. If the thesis is stated in the form of a question, it may be that a positive affirmation is lacking. Therefore, a simple declarative sentence is the most desirable type of thesis around which to build a speech.

As with all sentences, the thesis should have a subject and a predicate—a subject that is doing something with an object. The thesis suggested earlier has as its subject the clause "Our attempt to be gods," and as the predicate, "always ends in failure." Though that particular thesis is based upon the Genesis passage and could be the focus of a speech on idolatry, it can be improved upon even if we do not know what the speech will be in this formative stage. For one thing, it makes a statement, but it doesn't do anything. Any good speech should answer the questions How to? or So what? To affirm that our attempt to be godlike is doomed posits a correct biblical view, but we ought to know what that means for our lives, or how we can avoid idolatry, or what is the point of the whole thing other than announcing it.

Beyond that, the thesis has another fault. It is negative. The gospel is good news and a thesis should be affirmative.

Religious speaking should not be superficially happy; it should not smooth over rough places or sugarcoat serious matters. But the gospel does proclaim the good news of what God has done for us in Jesus Christ. That positive note of the gospel should underlie our Christian speaking.

Using the same example, this particular thesis has some good points. For example, it is short and clear. In addition, it has little jargon or technical language. A thesis like "God saves and redeems us through the blood of Jesus Christ" may say something theologically, but we need to be able to get beyond the language and put our thoughts in everyday speech. Otherwise, the speech itself will be filled with religious jargon, pious talk, and theological abstractions. When Jesus spoke, the people heard him gladly. That should be our aim as well.

Using the same thesis example once again, let us see if we can improve it in light of the discussion. Of course, it is somewhat difficult to do this unless the passage has been studied carefully and a specific speech is being constructed. Nevertheless, summarizing the discussion of the thesis, it is possible to make the statement more effective. Here is a better version: "When we accept our human limitations, we are free to relate to our fellow humans in God's name." The idea of accepting our limitations means that we shun idolatry, recognize God's sovereignty, and become aware of who we really are. The idea of relating to others is the predicate with an action step. It adds the call for *doing* something in light of the speech. An effective speech—especially a religious one—needs a claim in it. "Relating to our fellow humans" presupposes that the speaker will spell out what that means in light of God's acceptance of us. "In God's name" is our mandate. It would remind the speaker that there is the gospel—the good news. We do not relate to others just out of friendship or camaraderie. The Christian is one who recognizes his or her humanity under God. Therefore, the mandate is clear; we relate to all persons as brothers and sisters.

After the thesis of a speech has been formulated, the next step is building a clear outline. The outline is the blueprint, or skeleton of the speech. Its importance is similar to that of the thesis. The outline insures clarity, and that should be the first order of business in any effective speech. The person making a speech is not like an artist splashing colorful paint all over a canvas; he is more like a tour guide on a bus calling out the names of passing towns and special points of interest. There should be progression and movement in the speech and the outline insures that. Some speeches do not seem to be going anywhere, or else they go in circles. A speech should start somewhere and go somewhere. A beginning point and a destination are called for, and the outline is the basis for that journey.

Like the thesis, it should be simple. There is a difference between simplicity and simplemindedness. A good speaker, like a good actor (or a good anything else) is often disarming in his or her simplicity. Complexity and confusion usually reveal a confused mind. Ponderous or heavy ideas are often not profound; they are simply undigested. A good speaker strives for simplicity, and his outline is his insurance. Not only should it be simple and show movement, as we have indicated, but it should be readily apparent to the audience.

Some people make fun of preachers and speakers who have three points and a poem. Rightly so. Sameness can lead to staleness. However, the problem with the modern pulpit or platform is not overclarity; it is, rather, confusion. There is an old story told of a New England farmer who was shingling his barn in such a thick fog that he just shingled off into the fog. Too many speakers "shingle off into the fog." A clear outline is good insurance against fogginess and fuzziness.

Another way to look at the importance of the outline is to remind ourselves of three key words writers often keep in mind: *unity,* *coherence,* and *emphasis.* Unity is the concern with having one idea in the speech making sure that it is clear. The thesis is the best way to insure unity of the speech. It reminds us that the speech is not a detective playing "Point, point, who's got the point?" It is a revelation, not a concealment. Unity is basic to the speech; the thesis is its guarantee.

Coherence is, ideally, the result of how the speaker moves from one point to another in his speech. Many times we have heard speakers who finish one point and begin another without making a connection between them. It is as if a bridge has washed out, spilling us into a chasm and forcing us to climb up the other bank. A speech should flow from one point to another, make progress, and show logical connections. If a speaker is describing a trip from Chicago to St. Louis via Springfield, talking about Des Moines would be to detour logically as well as geographically. Or if a person is giving us five reasons why his Ford is better than a Chevrolet, and reason number four elaborates on a trip to Colorado, then this, too, is a hopeless detour. These examples may seem too absurd ever to occur, but similar problems do arise, even with so-called professional speakers.

To insure coherence, at least two steps can be taken. First, make sure the outline has a logical relationship. It can be simple as *problem* and *solution*. Or, it can state three ways in which a Christian can witness to his or her faith. Or, one could take a Bible passage and speak on it in the following order: (1) meaning (2) adaptation. Whatever the outline, the important thing is that it ''hang together,'' make sense, and show proper relationships. The second thing to do to help with coherence is to make sure that there are transition sentences between the various points. These are the ''bridges'' that help the speaker get from one point to the other and enable him or her to see whether the speech moves along clearly and smoothly. These may be the most important—if not the only—things a good speaker will need to write out. Leading the way out of the introduction, placed between each major point of the speech, and building to the conclusion, transition sentences are indispensable aids for clear and logical presentation.

Emphasis has to do with the amount of time spent on each major point. A good many speeches suffer from elephantiasis. They have a big trunk and body of beginning (especially with the problems of the world) and a little tail of conclusion (solutions for those problems). This is spending the wrong amount of time in the wrong places. If a person is talking about fear and the resources the Christian has to overcome that fear, an outline might be: (1) the fact of fear in our world, (2) the causes of that fear, and (3) the Christian answer to fear. If most of the speech is devoted to an introduction and the first two points, then the emphasis would be thrown off. The heart of that talk should be point three, and an outline should remind the speaker before the speech that the bulk of his time should be spent on the last point. One of the causes of unbalanced outlines is that it is easier to diagnose than prescribe. It is easier to talk about sin than grace. Bad news is more dramatic than good. Nevertheless, proper emphasis should be given to the thesis of the speech so that the speaker will not be majoring in the minors. In most cases, that will place the emphasis upon the positive affirmations of the speech.

At this point, the speech is well on its way. If a speaker has worked through the many possible ideas, selected one, formulated a thesis, and framed a clear outline, then the most difficult problems have been solved. Though a good deal of work remains, getting the idea refined and structured is so important that the speaker can have confidence at this juncture. The outline needs to be filled out, of course, like flesh fills out bone. Fleshing out the outline is adding support for the points made in the skeletal outline.

The support will take various forms. In *Principles of Speech*, Alan Monroe suggests seven of them. They are explanation; analogy, or comparison; illustration; specific instance; statistics; testimony; and restatement. Though there may be other ways of stating the kinds of support materials that build outlines, Monroe's will be sufficient for indicating the nature of the flesh that goes on the bones.

Explanation is simply what it suggests. One explains as clearly as possible what one is saying—both in ideas and in language. Of course, a whole speech is not explanation unless you are telling someone how to assemble a motor. But, an exposition of an idea is usually part of a speech.

Analogy, or comparison, usually relates the known to the unknown. For those speaking on religious subjects analogy is very important. In a way, our speaking about God is always analogical. We are trying to make the unknown, known; the abstract, concrete; the general, specific. To do those things, we use comparisons. "God's love is like . . ." Or, our analogies become more complex; they become parables. And thus the love of a father for his prodigal son becomes the love of God for prodigal humanity.

Illustration is usually a narrative or story. It is a way of making the material "come alive." In the next chapter we will spend more time on the illustration, but it is easy to see that an illustration will dramatize the points the speaker is trying to make.

Specific instance differs from illustration only in length. The narrative is left out. Instead of developing a longer illustration of the problem of hunger in our day, a specific instance might do as well and be just as vivid. "One half the world's population is going to bed hungry tonight" would be a specific instance.

Statistics means using numbers to support a point. They will not be in every speech, nor should they be. But when used, they can be arresting. The one on hunger above is such a statistic. Rather than reading a table of numbers, one vivid statistic can be memorable.

Testimony is using statements on the lives of others. In religious speaking, Jesus and his teachings are used in this way. Authorities are quoted in speeches to great effect, depending upon the type of speech and on the credibility of the one quoted.

Restatement simply means saying the same thing in another way. We usually think of the conclusion doing that, but the thesis of a speech may have a recurring emphasis in the speech by dramatizing it in different ways.

Support, such as these examples, will be the kinds of material that amplify a brief outline form into a more highly developed speech. Moving from the idea to the thesis to the outline and to the development of the outline will enable the speaker to get a firm grasp on the material. Thus, one is able to be articulate in front of one's listeners. Nothing could be more important or more necessary in the communication of ideas.

In summary: The building of an effective speech—religious or otherwise—has several indispensable steps.

1. Each speech should have a clearly stated *thesis* that is a one-sentence kernel of the entire speech. With that formulated, the speech will have clarity. Without a thesis, confusion reigns.

2. Since the gospel is at least the communication of an idea, the speech on a religious theme should certainly make sense. The thesis insures that meaning is communicated.

3. A good speech will have a clear outline underneath that provides the blueprint for the unfolding of the speaker's ideas. It follows from the thesis and insures the clarity and progression of the speaker's thoughts.

4. *Unity, coherence,* and *emphasis* are three keys by which

to check the clarity of an outline. If these three are taken seriously, the outline will usually be effective.

5. The outline will need more than "bare bones." It will need flesh. Among the forms of support that give substance to the "skeletal" ideas are explanation, illustration, statistics, analogy, testimony, specific instance, and restatement.

6. No one would purport to speak for God unless he or she has ideas that are clearly thought out and then articulated effectively. The outline is the most basic step in that whole process.

6

Getting It All Together
(Developing the Idea)

Walter Lippmann reportedly once said that "people think with pictures in their heads." If so, that motto should be placed on the study walls of speakers along with "Think" and "Pray." Nothing could help the speaker more than to remember the effectiveness of combining visual with oral communication.

At this particular point in the development of the speech, the importance of dramatization will be seen most clearly. We have demonstrated how a speech grows from the development of an idea into a specific thesis, then branches into an outline. The steps involved in finishing the speech before delivery are concerned with visualization and dramatization.

Take, for example, the introduction. Some might suppose it strange that the introduction is not the first thing accomplished in building a speech. Actually, it could be. Some speakers write the introduction first in order to "get things going." There are strong reasons, however, for giving the introduction special and intense concern after the outline has been completed. For one thing, its importance cannot be overemphasized. The first few minutes of a speech may determine its outcome. There is a kind of wrestling match between audience and speaker over who is going to control

71

attention for the remaining minutes of the speech. That introduction—even the first sentence—may determine the outcome of the entire speech. Another reason, and close to the first, is that although the introduction is obviously related to the speech itself, it has other functions and needs specific treatment.

The functions of an introduction can best be seen by emphasizing two "musts" for a good introduction. First, it should open, or lead into, the speech by raising clearly the subject or topic under discussion. Though they may seem obvious, many speeches fail dismally at this very point. Some speakers feel compelled to begin a speech with a couple of stories to "loosen up" the group. Or, they may try to get the audience's attention by relating a humorous incident having nothing to do with the speech. Such approaches—however interesting—are faults that should be avoided in an introduction.

To raise distinctly the topic under discussion is another way of assuring that the introduction will be integrally related to the speech. It should open up the subject and lead into the speech. If it does not do that, it fails. If it does that, it is at least halfway effective. Let's pick up the passage referred to in the last chapter, Genesis 11:1-9. As was suggested there, the theme for that scripture lesson could be idolatry. An introduction to that speech, sermon, or meditation should surely introduce idolatry. Remember again that the thesis differs from the subject or theme. The topic, theme, or subject is idolatry. The thesis finally developed in the earlier discussion was "When we accept our human limitations, we are free to relate to our fellow humans in God's name." That thesis would not normally come in the introduction (though it could), but the subject idolatry certainly would.

The second "must" for an effective introduction is that it command the audience's attention. Earlier it was suggested that the first few minutes of a speech may amount to the most important part of the speech. Special care in getting the attention of the audience recognizes the importance of the beginning. We have long heard that the beginning and the end of a speech naturally have the attention of an audience. To recognize this fact enables one to take seriously the time demanded in arousing the interest of the listeners.

How do we secure attention from a congregation? First of all, we need to remember that the two functions of getting attention and opening up the speech are complementary and must be seen in that way. We do not seek attention for its own sake, nor should we see the subject matter of the speech as distinct from the way that the attention has been secured. In other words, the introduction has a purpose, a purpose that has these two important parts. Remembering that, we can consider several effective ways by which attention can be grasped.

One way is to begin with an arresting statement. For example, the assertion "One half of the population of the world is going to bed hungry tonight" (a statement used earlier to illustrate the principle of specific instance) would be effective for opening up a talk on the problem of world hunger. If such an opening statement is true, if it leads legitimately into the speech and does not have only shock value, then it is a most effective way to arouse interest.

Or, similarly, an arresting quotation would make an

effective beginning. Lines such as the following from Robert Frost's "Road Not Taken" are a good example:

> Two roads diverged in a wood, and I—
> I took the one less traveled by,
> And that has made all the difference.

If used to introduce a theme that called upon Christians not to follow the crowd, such a quotation would not only serve to evoke interest but would get to the heart of the subject. One caution, however, is that the quotation should not be too long and should not be read from notes. Part of what makes an effective beginning is physical directness. Thus a brief quotation committed to memory and delivered by looking straight at the audience can have real impact.

Questions are another effective means of opening a speech. "Have you ever considered what the world would be like without the church?" Such a question could well begin a speech on the importance of the Christian church in our lives. The caution in regard to questions is not to raise too many and thus "scare up more rabbits than you are able to shoot." Even worse would be to raise a question or questions that are not dealt with in the following remarks.

Dialogue can be an exciting way to begin a speech. Even a hypothetical or imaginary dialogue is permissible if it does not do an injustice to the truth. For example, a speaker might imagine a brief conversation between a husband and a wife in order to set up a talk on family or marriage problems. Even biblical materials can be used this way. Paul's defense before Festus and King Agrippa in Acts 26 could be handled effectively as dialogue. This kind of a beginning can be very dramatic. But, that can also be a danger. There is a difference between being dramatic and being theatrical. The latter is to be avoided. Such concerns as soft lights, assuming different roles, costuming, and generally turning the speech into a performance normally should not invade the speech-event. The use of dialogue, though, strengthened by mere suggestion of the various characters involved and presented with directness and strong eye contact can have a very impressive effect. Here again, though, the length should be kept within bounds. This kind of material has a way of expanding and distorting the emphasis of the talk even before getting to the body of the speech.

Some religious speakers wonder if all speeches should begin with biblical material, especially a text. Some preachers affirm they should. Religious speeches—even sermons—do not need to begin with texts to make them either biblical or religious. All of the examples given above could be followed by strictly biblical material. On the other hand, a text in itself could arrest attention and arouse interest if it had those qualities. "No one can serve two masters. . . . You cannot serve God and mammon" (Matt. 6:24) could put before any audience the choice between the Christian way of life and the ways of this world; or, it could dramatize the importance of single-mindedness for the committed Christian.

Though there are many other ways a speech may begin, these are some of the most common. An introduction that arrests attention and leads into the subject cannot be a total loss. Indeed, faithful attention to arousing the interest of the audience and from there arresting its attention and leading it

75

into the speech itself are the hallmarks of effective introduction. Those two rules, plus brevity, will save speakers from many speech pitfalls. Most introductions are too long any way, and given the tendency to "set the stage" in the beginning of a speech, the aorta may develop an aneurysm even before the speaker is into the body of the talk. Most speakers do need to get started promptly.

If the beginning of the speech is the most important part of the whole enterprise, the conclusion cannot be far behind. The audience perks up there, as well as at the start. It is easy to test this if the speaker wants to run the risk. Any time a speaker says, "In conclusion" or "Finally," the members of the audience look up expectantly, begin to reach for the children's coats, and feel around for their umbrellas. After those words, or their equivalent, have been uttered, the speaker had better quit. Otherwise, the people will assume he is like the little boy who cried wolf, and they won't take him seriously the next time.

To say that the conclusion should end the speech ought to be enough advice for any speaker, but many speakers have trouble stopping. Consider the preacher whose wife told him—after a sermon which seemed to be forever ending— "Dear, you missed several good opportunities to stop this morning." Ending the speech effectively may take more care than would seem appropriate, but a proper conclusion can give a speech tremendous impact.

There are several options open to the speaker. One is to summarize the speech. Earlier, in building the speech, we talked of restatement as a form of support. The conclusion can be a restatement of the major points in the speech or of the thesis itself. Suppose a speech were being prepared on three values of the Christian life and the major points were (1) the Christian comes to terms with God; (2) the Christian comes to terms with self; (3) the Christian comes to terms with others. The conclusion could be a simple restatement of those three points. While not very dramatic, the conclusion would register high on the clarity scale, and that is not to be despised.

The conclusion could also make an application. Some teaching or truth that has been raised in the speech could be applied to some specific situation. A speech on God's love and forgiveness could be made vivid in the conclusion by making an analogy to a human situation.

> Suppose you know a family situation in which there has been unfaithfulness on the part of the husband. The wife is brokenhearted, the children distressed, and the husband remorseful. There is little the husband can do to restore the marital relationship, even though he is repentant and asks forgiveness. He cannot buy his way back with flowers, candy, or mink coats. Only if the wife decides to forgive him can the relationship be restored, for the heart of forgiveness is giving. The wife does forgive, and the family is brought together again. So does God's love and forgiveness restore us.

The conclusion can also motivate to action. A speech on brotherhood that has attacked racism, appealed for goodwill among all groups, and encouraged Christian people to take a stand and work for specific solutions could very well conclude by asking the audience to get involved in working for open housing in the community.

These three examples in no way exhaust the multiplicity of

options open to the speaker in constructing conclusions. One of the most effective is a conclusion that dramatizes the thesis. It lifts up the thesis (or the basic affirmation of the sermon) and restates it through a story, poem, dramatic incident, quotation, or arresting sentence. In many ways, this conclusion combines summary, application, and motivation. It "wraps up" the whole sermon in capsule form and ends the speech with an impact.

All examples of introductions, conclusions, and illustrations, are difficult to understand outside the context of the speech, but some are worth considering. In a sermon on the wedding feast at Cana (John 2:1-11), the thesis was, "Just as Jesus Christ brings new life (water into wine), so too can we have new life—again and again." The sermon concluded: "Christ comes to our 'wedding feasts'—schools, lives, jobs, relationships—and turns the water of our old selves into the wine of new spirits, with fresh beginnings and new life."

In another religious speech with the title "He Took A Towel," the thesis was, "Jesus calls us to service in the common routine of life." That particular speech ended: "Herman Hesse in his book *Journey to the East* tells a mythical story of a group of men making a pilgrimage to the East. With them is a servant named Leo who does their menial chores, sustains them with his spirit and song, and, by the quality of his presence, lifts them above what they would otherwise be. Then he disappears; the group falls apart; and the journey is abandoned. One of the group—after many years of wandering on his own—finds Leo, and, of all things, discovers that Leo is the head of the Order, the noble leader, the goal of their quest. Long before Herman Hesse, we

Christians knew that our Lord and Master was also the Suffering Servant. And that legacy becomes ours as we live out our lives together.''

Go back to the Tower of Babel lesson with the subject idolatry and the thesis ''When we accept our human limitations, we are free to relate to our fellow humans in God's name.'' Since we have the scripture passage, a possible subject, and a tentative thesis—but no speech—a good practice is to look at the thesis and see what kind of a conclusion might develop along the lines that have been discussed. Of course, one would naturally have ready the outline and thesis of speech before the introduction and conclusion, but an exercise in conclusion building would not be amiss. How could you go about dramatizing that thesis if it were yours?

The final item to be considered in fleshing out the speech before delivery is the matter of illustration. We have seen earlier that an illustration is, most importantly, a form of support that illuminates or dramatizes a point being made. The illustration should throw light on that point, not on itself. If the audience goes away remembering the illustration and not its point, then the illustration has failed. Occasionally a speaker will be tempted to tell a good story he or she has heard whether it fits into the speech or not. Speakers should resist that temptation. The illustration opens the window on the point being made. If it does that, it succeeds; otherwise, it fails.

Among other things, this means that the illustration should develop from the point being made and not dangle from the speech outline like a bauble on a Christmas tree. One occasionally hears speeches in which illustrations are strung onto the general theme like a necklace of many colored beads. The speech seems to be a collection of stories surrounding a vague idea. A speech whose aim is to communicate a certain idea will have more substance than that, and a well-conceived outline is the best insurance against developing a talk with "stories." The speaker will ask the question What is the best way to illuminate this idea? From that starting point the illustration will develop naturally.

Illustrations should also have the touch of universality about them. Simply put, an illustration should touch the basic hungers of the heart of all people. The story of a child starving in India will reach the heart of a mother in Indiana because of the love of mothers for children everywhere. A Robert Frost poem can involve people who have never seen birch trees, snowy woods, or rock fences, because he is writing about concerns that affect all of us. An illustration should do that; and if it does, it can derive from a speaker's reading, the newspaper, or his or her personal experiences.

It is this last—the personal element of illustration—that needs special attention. The personal illustration—in which the speaker is the actual subject—may be both the best and most dangerous kind. Positively, of course, that which is closest to us will have the most authenticity and the strongest link to reality. If we are telling of an incident that happened to us, then surely that will be strong support, good proof, and fortification for our ethos with the audience.

On the other hand, personal illustrations can affect the speech adversely. Some speakers—without even knowing it—can be the heroes of their illustrations. They dramatize themselves, not the ideas. They solve someone's problem; they tell of their families' accomplishments; they bear witness to their own faith—time and again. Their testimony and witness—overdone—may point to them more than to the ideas or even to the gospel itself. So, judiciously used, a personal illustration is excellent; without careful use, it can be a disaster.

One other thing. The effective speaker will "dig up" his own illustrations rather than depend upon books of quotations, snappy sayings, or helps for hungry speakers. Illustrations that are your own, that are the results of your reading and your experience, will sound better and be more authentic when given in a speech. Time spent in reading widely will be more profitable than looking for "canned" illustrations that may be old, hackneyed, and overused. New speakers are tempted to lean on others for help in getting started. <u>Above all, never tell a story that happened to someone else as if it happened to you. That is dishonest and will destroy your ethos.</u> Better for the speech to be clear and unadorned than filled with trite stories that have been making the banquet circuit for a quarter of a century. Mine your own gold; it will shine brighter because you found it.

Getting it all together means that the speech has been readied for delivery through visualization and dramatization of thesis and outline.

In summary: Several things should be kept in mind as you put the finishing touches on the speech.

1. Nothing could be more important for the speaker to

remember than the necessity of dramatizing the ideas in the speech.

2. The introduction dramatizes the idea in two important ways—arresting attention and introducing the subject to be discussed as succinctly as possible.

3. The most effective conclusion dramatizes the thesis of the speech.

4. The major concern of the illustrations of a speech is to illustrate the idea being presented, not themselves.

7

Hey, Look Me Over
(Delivering the Speech: Visible)

Many good speeches never get off the ground. There doesn't seem to be enough "wing power" to get them soaring into the air. How many times have we heard speakers who simply cannot speak well? Whether it is making an announcement at a board meeting, introducing a speaker at a luncheon club, or standing up on Lay Person's Day at the church, the presentation is often ineffective. Usually it is due to poor delivery. Yet, with some effort, all of us can improve this aspect of our speaking.

In a way it is impossible to be too dogmatic about the delivery of a speech. There are so many varied ways of speaking well, so many speakers who differ widely in their approach, that there seems no one way that will be fitting for all. Yet there are certain principles all of us can follow as we seek to be better on our feet. The important thing to remember is that delivery and content are integrally related. Many times a poor delivery will be the result of a fuzzy or a vague idea. A confusing idea and an ineffective outline will result in a confused delivery. And, on the other hand, a well-ordered speech can fail because of poor enunciation, an unpleasant voice, or even bad posture.

Some speakers minimize the importance of delivery. They contend that if they have a good idea, the delivery will take

83

care of itself. As long as you have something to say, it doesn't matter much how you say it. The problem with this philosophy is that the audience doesn't think that way. They listen to the speech as a whole. To them the delivery, content, structure, and ideas are all wrapped up in a single package. It is a speech-event. They may react negatively to an entire speech because of an ineffective delivery. They might not be conscious of the reason, but a poor voice may ruin the whole speech for them—no matter how good the ideas.

Speakers—even experienced ones—are tempted to believe they are pretty good on their feet. Sometimes an aptitude for being at ease on one's feet will delude us into thinking that because we are not frightened, we are effective. New speakers, too, may feel they need little help in delivery, especially if the few times they have spoken they have gotten positive feedback from the audience. The experienced speaker may have developed some bad speech habits but be oblivious to them because he or she has had no one criticize his or her work. Also, a person who has tasted the "heady wine" of speech making, has seemingly held an audience in the palm of his hand, and had people say at the end, "Great!" may have problems listening to advice about delivering a speech. Nevertheless, an effective speaker—experienced or new—will work as hard to be as competent in delivery as in content.

Was it the old carnival barker who said, while pointing to the prizes lining his booth, "What you see is what you get"? In speaking it is the same. What the audience sees before them in the speaker affects the speech and their response to it—even before the speaker opens his or her mouth.

84

Take posture, for example. Before the speech begins, the posture may be "speaking." If the speaker begins by slouching on the podium or collapsing all over the pulpit or holding onto the speaker's stand for dear life, then something has already been communicated even before his mouth has opened. While a rigid and formal posture would connote a stiff person—if not a stiff speech—the overrelaxed posture will do the reverse. A speaker who is too casual will give the impression that the speech is casual as well, thus lowering the threshold of the audience's expectancy.

A speech teacher once said to me that a speaker should stand with one foot in front of the other, balancing the weight on the balls of the feet as if suspended from the ceiling by a piano wire, hands at the sides. As a matter of fact, this is a comfortable position. But there is no one best posture. The speaker should be comfortable before the group and should not be distracting. The beginning posture is especially important. There is nothing wrong with a hand in the pocket or a gentle lean on the podium or even a relaxed body. Any of these postures at the outset, though, may set the tone for the entire speech. If the speaker begins with a comfortable stance, looking directly at the audience, then there is plenty of latitude for a variety of bodily action throughout the speech.

Bodily action or gestures also present problems for speakers. The best motto for bodily action is found in a line from *Annie Get Your Gun:* "Doin' what comes naturally." An effective speaker will normally make gestures without thinking, and the ideas and mood of the speech will dictate the gestures. "Being natural" needs some restraint, of course. There are two primary cautions concerning gestures that should be kept in mind.

First of all, the mood should determine the action. That is, a gesture is an external action determined by an internal thought or idea. A good speaker would not be talking about love and at the same time pound the podium with a fist. On the other hand, a clenched fist might be appropriate if the emotion to be portrayed is anger. While there are many rules for gesturing, including matching the appropriate gesture with a particular mood, the natural gesture will probably come of its own accord in most cases. A speaker might occasionally make a check of gestures by practicing speaking in front of a full-length mirror. Such an exercise—to be done only rarely—would enable the speaker to see if the gestures are appropriate to the mood of the speech.

The second caution concerning gestures has to do with whether they are distracting or not. For example, a large sweeping gesture made at the beginning of a speech for no apparent reason would be distracting. In the old-time melodramas, part of what was so comic was the separation of word and action. The heroine would say to the villain, "Go, and never darken my door again." Then, after a pause, she would point to the door. In a speech, a gesture not tied to word or mood, while not comic, may be distracting. An overabundance of bodily action can communicate nervousness to the audience. Better the energy go into voice, delivery, and ideas than into unmotivated gestures.

Distracting as superfluous gestures may be, it is much easier to curb them than it is to generate movement in a person who has little or no dynamism. A person who gestures too much can at least lock his hands behind his back, put his hands in his pockets or grasp the podium. The person with no gestures has a more difficult problem; for gestures ultimately have to come from within. The way to achieve this is to practice bodily action that will say visually what the ideas are saying. Here again, with caution, an occasional practice session before a mirror can help the person who is not letting the action dramatize the tone and feelings of the ideas.

Facial expressions are just as important. The psalmist said that as a man thought in his heart so he was. In terms of speaking, the face may be the most revealing of all. The key to one's internality may be through the facial expressions. An expressive face that is consonant with the ideas being expressed can be tremendously effective in creating audience receptivity. Conversely, a deadpan expression or an expression at variance with what is being uttered can defeat a speaker's purpose.

Take two extremes as examples. Here is a speaker who has a very expressive face with a warm, infectious smile. That smile holds the promise of a friendly, concerned human being. Since the face and person are integral, that would be natural. The only problem would be if the warm and friendly smile were always there, notwithstanding the subject matter. It is one thing to have the support of the voice, manner, and face when talking about tenderness, love, or family. It is quite another to be talking about the seriousness of the world's hunger problem and then break into a beatific smile. The face needs to fit the material and an oversmiling person, as in this example, might inadvertently suggest that he or she is not taking the material seriously.

The other extreme is the deadpan. Many speakers have a face that is going to waste. No matter what they talk about—whether love, joy, anger, war, or whatever—the face remains strangely immobile. They react to their subject matter and the various portions of their speech identically. Various subject matter should cause a variety of responses in our own beings as speakers, and even within a speech on a single subject there will be a variety of climaxes. The introduction, conclusions, and illustrations will all have more arresting and dramatic content than the parts of a speech that are simply explanation. Those various portions should be reflected in our voices, gestures, and faces.

Achieving mobility in the face or curbing the occasional overabundance of facial reactions are both remedied in the same way. The key is to remember the connection between the material of the speech and the reaction to it in delivery. The person with a deadpan expression for all occasions may consciously need to work on learning to show emotions outwardly. One young speaker with this problem would stand in front of a mirror and attempt to register various emotions. He would think of love, hate, anger, tenderness, and then attempt to portray them in his face. That might be too mechanical for most of us, but some attention to monitoring our own emotional reactions to our content will be helpful in our speaking. The same may be said of the overexpressive face, or the speaker with the too-ready smile (or the too-ready frown). The face should be the barometer of a speech's emotional content. If one can escape the pitfall of mechanical manipulation, one's face can be a boon to one's speaking. Occasional practice in front of a mirror, a session in front of a

video tape machine, a visit to a local speech teacher, or some
candid help from a friend are all ways that we can test our
reactions to our material.

Eye contact is in reality tied in with facial expression. The
eyes are part of the same barometer that affects the face in
regard to the material and the words of a speech. On the other
hand, the eyes have special significance in the delivery of a
speech. How does one look at the audience? Does one look at
it directly?

Some speakers have been taught that when addressing an
audience they should look at an imaginary spot just above the
audience's heads, since this will give the impression of
looking at the audience as a whole. Other speakers look away
from the audience—at a spot on the wall, out the window, or
down at the podium. Sometimes the faraway look signals a
dramatic pause or a gathering of one's thoughts. But often it
reveals a fear of looking at the audience diectly. Looking
down can be a result of the same fear, but more often it shows
that the speaker is bound to the notes or manuscript he has
brought with him to the podium.

The best thing for a speaker to remember in regard to eye
contact is a line from *The Ancient Mariner:* "He holds him
with his glittering eye." Put more simply, we should look
upon an audience as a collection of individual persons. This
does not mean we should go chair by chair and row by row
through an entire twenty-minute speech glancing at everyone.
Nor does it mean we should find a friendly face and stay with
it, or spend a lot of time with a frowning face trying to
change the look. We should keep in mind that we are persons

speaking to other persons, and we should address all of them accordingly—with our eyes.

The person who is afraid to look at the audience may have a problem that goes beyond speaking. If he cannot remedy the normal nervousness that accompanies the thrill of speaking, he may have deeper problems requiring the professional attention of a minister or psychologist. As suggested earlier, normal stage fright can be overcome.

Looking down due to notes—or even reading within the speech—will be dealt with in the next chapter. At this point, one should be reminded that anything that breaks contact with the audience is to be avoided. When the speaker looks down, he loses the attention of the audience; and the audience, in turn, may focus their attention in another direction. An illustration that has to be read, a poem that is read rather than quoted, or even a Bible that is picked up within a speech—all of these, no matter how worthwhile they may be for other reasons, run the risk of interrupting contact with the audience and thereby losing its interest. The speaker cannot be reminded too often or too strongly that what commands attention determines action. The speaker should remember that the entire speech demands the utmost in his or her skills to keep the attention of the audience. The eyes are one of the most important ways that that can be done.

In summary, the speaker is "speaking" even before he opens his mouth to utter a single word. The way we walk into the meeting, how we sit, and how we participate in the opening proceedings are all part of the speech-event. And, before and during the speech itself, we will be communicating through our posture, our bodily action, our faces, and our eyes. Indeed, what we are saying in these ways may be stronger than what we are saying in the speech itself. These nonvocal aspects of our speech are part of what we have called our ethos—that part of us that may work adversely or positively in terms of the audience's response. If what we are doing with these functions does not distract from, and is consonant with, the content and tone of the speech, then our speech will be supported with effectiveness. Several of the points need to be remembered:

1. Content and delivery are inseparable. The good speaker will be adequate in both areas. Weakness in one or the other can ruin a speech.

2. Delivery cannot be minimized and needs the same care and seriousness that belongs to the content, structure, and style of the speech.

3. Posture, bodily action, facial expressions, and eye contact are functions of the nonvocal aspects of speaking that will communicate either negatively or positively.

4. Concern for delivery effectiveness coupled with attention to disciplined work through criticism, practice, minimal techniques, and use of readily available audio-visual equipment will enable the dedicated speaker to improve his speech skills.

8

Sound Off!
(Delivering the Speech: Audible)

It was said of George Whitefield that he could bring tears to his audience's eyes by the way he pronounced "Mesopotamia." Most of us do not have the gifts of this great eighteenth-century evangelist, but we can do a great deal with the voices we have. What is *heard* is just as important as what is *seen;* therefore, Christian speakers should lay their voices and delivery, as well as their hearts, on the altar of commitment.

We have referred repeatedly to the importance of our *ethos*—that persuasion which arises out of our being, our personhood, our selves. Nothing we do will be more important than what we radiate from our total presence in front of an audience. The response of our audiences will be determined in large part by what they "feel" about us as they hear us speak. Much of their feeling will be undefined, unclear, and impressionistic; yet, they will make judgments about our speech, sometimes without knowing why. The use of the voice will be one of these areas that will cause both negative and positive responses. Just as audiences are unaware of their reasons for liking or disliking a speech, speakers are often unaware of the importance of their delivery in getting a favorable response.

Whether we like it or not, the person with the deep,

resonant voice will be "making points" with the audience, since people tend to respond positively to a pleasant voice. Conversely, the person with the high, squeaky unpleasant voice will be getting an unfavorable initial response from the audience. In the first instance, the speaker may dissipate all of that goodwill if the content is poor. Saying nothing well is to no avail. And, the person with the unpleasant speaking voice may overcome the poor voice by virtue of the content. The important thing to realize is that our voices and delivery are vitally connected to the content of our speeches and will affect intensely the response.

There are at least four things that make for effective vocal delivery, and there is nothing magical about a single one of them. They are proper breathing, an open throat, resonance, and articulation. Basic to all is proper breathing. The world's future does not hang on "belly breathing" by any means, but the foundation for a good voice is the support that comes through proper breathing. Most of us are shallow breathers, who have been taught from the earliest gym classes or the army to throw back our shoulders, throw out our chests, and suck in our stomachs. That may be a great way to win a war or improve posture, but it doesn't help much in speaking. Support for speaking comes from deep breathing, which fills the lungs, enlarges the diaphramatic region of the body, and pushes out the stomach. It is almost the reverse of sucking in the stomach and breathing shallowly through the chest. A baby crying, a dog panting, a miler racing, or diva singing will all reveal naturally the breathing that results from the physical exertion of the midsection.

Proper breathing gives support to the voice, helps it find its optimum pitch, prevents it from becoming breathy, and even goes a long way towards controlling stage fright. Beginning with the breathing mechanism, there are several options for the person seeking to improve his voice. He can get a speech book from the local library, look up the chapter on voice production, and follow the exercises outlined for achieving proper breathing. Or, he can get in touch with a speech teacher or voice coach at a local or nearby school. After one or two interviews, he will undoubtedly be on the road to self-improvement. A serious student of speaking will not begrudge a modest investment of time and money in order to achieve effectiveness in this serious business of speaking and witnessing to others. A friend who is an experienced speaker can also be of help. But, there is much one can do alone. Reading aloud, for example, is one of the best ways to develop the voice.

Without attempting to give a full-blown voice lesson, a brief example might suffice to show the way one might proceed—with or without help. Stretch out on your back, on a flat surface like a floor or bed. Close your eyes and relax. Then take a deep breath by letting your lungs fill up with air and enlarge the body cavity and push against the belt. When the lungs are filled, the chest cavity full, and the stomach area enlarged all around the belt area, hold the breath for a moment, and then let it out slowly. Keep this rhythm going, and you will see that this is not always the "natural" way we breathe. In fact, you may feel light-headed briefly as you take in fresh air and expand your lungs.

After getting the rhythm of breathing in and out and holding the breath out against the belt, say something like

"Ho" or "Halt." What is said should cause movement in the stomach equivalent to what is being said with the voice. When that is achieved, so is the principle. And, as the air goes out, the stomach seems pressed against the backbone. When another breath is taken, the lungs fill again. One might picture a balloon filled with air, but not knotted, from which air escapes freely as one pushes it out. In the case of breathing, though, the lungs are never empty, and a great reservoir of breath remains. This reservoir of air is what gives support to the voice, prevents the breathiness that can occur due to nervousness, and helps keep the voice at its proper pitch and range.

Now, having tried this relaxation and breathing process, one is ready to practice reading aloud, one of the best ways to help speaking of any kind. Stand in an empty sanctuary or large Sunday school room at your local church. At the pulpit or lectern, stand straight but relaxed. Breathe deeply for a few minutes, and then begin. Read something like a psalm, read very slowly, and attempt to make an imaginary person on the back row hear your words. Do this without shouting or forcing the voice. Do it by letting the voice project by the power that comes from underneath it.

The other three items of vocal production should be mentioned here; for they are also helped through reading aloud. An open throat is the second factor in the vocal mechanism that carries weight in regard to quality. It simply means that the throat is not constricted and that the airstream and sound waves issue from the mouth unimpeded. We have all heard the tight, flat, constricted voice that seems to originate from the throat. An open throat is the antidote for these unpleasant qualities we often hear. The most important way in which this quality is reached is through the proper breathing described above. When one breathes deeply, the body is more relaxed, the throat mechanism is released from constriction, and the throat seems open.

The third quality is also affected by proper breathing. Resonance is achieved when the voice vibrates throughout the head as if it were a sounding box. The sound does not come through the nasal passages alone, nor just the mouth, but vibrates throughout the head. Humming is a good way to test the resonance of one's voice. Here again, the breath control we have described will be an invaluable aid to the resonance of the voice. In short, proper breathing gives support to the voice, helps with the proper pitch, opens the throat, and aids in resonance.

The fourth item, articulation, does not depend as much on proper breathing, but it is no less important. Most of us have lazy lips, tight jaws, or sluggish tongues when it comes to speaking distinctly. We can get through the day conversing with friends or business partners in partial sentences, grunts, nods, and mushy diction. When it comes to speaking, though, all of these qualities affect the speech adversely. Enunciating words clearly is a must for an effective speaker. Loudspeaker systems have allowed us to get by with sloppy speaking; for they can amplify the voice enough to be heard no matter what its faults. Reading aloud with the determination to pronounce each syllable of each word distinctly is the most effective way to strengthen diction. We need to open our mouths wider, make our jaws flexible, tighten our lips, and loosen our lazy tongues. Determined practice with precise reading of printed material will go a long way towards strengthening the diction of a speaker. The speaker's rate of speaking—whether fast or slow—is not so important if the diction is sharp and clean.

There are, of course, many items that make for effective delivery besides breathing, open throat, resonance, and articulation. A speaker needs to sound forceful without having to shout, but the qualities we have mentioned should result in effective forcefulness. A voice should have melody. Melody refers to the quality of variety within the vocal range. Occasionally one hears a speaker who talks in a monotone. This is a Johnny-one-note kind of speech, in which the words arrive at the same rate and on the same pitch all through the talk. Boredom results. The other extreme is the overdone melody, in which the entire vocal range is explored. This speaking is filled with extreme emphases— even when talking about minor matters. Making serious matters sound pompous or light matters sound serious is a ludicrous exercise. Such speaking often besets the clergy person, who becomes stilted and over formal when he or she talks from the pulpit. If you find yourself adopting a different manner of speaking when entering a speech situation, there may be cause for alarm.

We hear a great deal about *conversational* speaking, and that term is fraught with both good and bad aspects. As seen above, much of our day-by-day speaking is semiarticulate; it is overrun with gesture and often too softly or slovenly enunciated. When this colloquial style is carried over to a speech situation—even amplified—then such speaking, though labeled conversational, will have negative results.

Speech should be articulate, forceful, and easily understood; and if it takes place before an audience it should have power and energy. On the other hand, there are certain qualities of conversational speech that are indispensable to good speaking. The chief of these is the rhythm of conversation. That is, a speaker before an audience should be speaking as a real person talking to other real persons. The speech should have the sound of honest talk. A person should not be essentially different from what he or she would be in other situations. Natural human talk before an audience should be in the form of discourse, but it should be human talk that is highly energized, articulate, and filled with honest emotion.

The phrase *honest emotion* raises one of the most important and most dangerous concepts of the speech-event. Most of us are nervous about the term *emotion* in connection with speaking. Yet our emotions are part of our beings, as are our minds, hearts, and spirits. We have talked a great deal about the importance of ideas, clarity, outlines, and communication of meaning. All of that needs emphasis. But when we hear a speech, we also hear a person; and that person is part of what he says. Here comes ethos again. The emotional, the nonvocal aspects of speaking, are all part of the communication process. That total event will radiate our total personhood as we speak, and emotions are part of that package.

 The problem with emotion is that we confuse emotion with emotionalism. Most of us react negatively to the tear-jerking evangelist, the high-pressure salesman, or the bombastic politician. Corny stories designed to "get to us" stick out like sore thumbs. We have a built-in protection against the propagandists who try to plumb our depths and elicit cheap responses. Rightly so! However, our emotions are part of us; and though we should be wary of cheap feelings, we should be concerned with the true, human emotions that are part of our lives. We should not be afraid to let those be a part of our speeches. If we are moved or feel deeply about our subject, then there is no reason that emotion should not be part of the speech.

The main concern for our speech is to communicate the idea, of course, but the feeling tone will be an important part of that communication. We cannot build fervor where there is none; it must come from within ourselves and our material. Apart from our own fear of ''letting go,'' sometimes our speeches do not have enough life because we have put too much on paper. As we shall see, that can be a barrier to the effectiveness of our delivery. In this instance, it also can be a barrier to revealing our feelings. If we can react honestly to our subject matter, underplay rather than overplay our emotions, and focus on the ideas, then the speaker should not feel guilty about the feeling tone he expresses. Indeed, it will be indispensable to the speech.

The last—and perhaps most important—factor in the presentation of a speech is the method used to deliver it. How can the prepared speech be delivered most effectively? Speakers vary in their methods, and no one method will suffice for everybody every time. Still there are some strengths and weaknesses in the various ways speakers present their materials. There are generally three methods that are most persistently used by speakers: (1) memorization, (2) written to be read, and (3) extemporaneous.

The first method, memorization, has some advantages, but it has a great many more disadvantages. Assuming that the basic outline is finished—which is an indispensable step—some speakers go on to write out the speech word for word. Then they take the manuscript, go over it many times, consciously commit it to memory, and then deliver its contents to the audience without the help of notes.

This method seems to be compelling. Writing out a speech has certain distinct advantages. For one thing, it requires fleshing out the outline, and this, in turn, ensures the speech will have sufficient preparation. That preparation will not only aid the speaker, but it will give the audience the impression that the speaker is well prepared. In turn, that will increase his ethos, or credibility. Further, a written speech helps one to concentrate on style. The language will be more carefully chosen, the mistakes fewer, and the ideas couched more felicitously. Beyond that, a memorized speech enables the speaker to maintain continuous eye contact with the audience.

In spite of these apparent advantages, however, the disadvantages are sufficient to give caution to anyone who contemplates speaking by the method of memorization. For one thing, unless one has a photographic mind—if there is such a thing—committing a speech to memory can be a time-consuming endeavor. To contemplate spending one's life—even as a part-time speaker—trying to memorize speeches can be a burden that needs to be measured against its results. Another problem is that the speech written out to be memorized often puts its emphasis upon style rather than ideas. Many of us are unable to write as we speak; therefore, the speech sounds more like a work of literature than an informal address. Those are two different modes of discourse. Above all, memorization often places the speaker in a mental and oral straitjacket. A person may memorize the speech, focus on the memorization during the presentation, and be unable to adapt to on-the-spot ideas, reactions from the audience, or the out-of-the ordinary things that occasionally happen during a speaking event. Unless one has a facility for memorization and a thoroughly oral style of writing, the memorization method can lock the speaker into an inflexible pattern of speech that lacks the spontaneity one strives for in communication.

In terms of advantages and disadvantages, the writing of a speech to be read is a method of delivery similar to the memorized speech. The same advantages of careful preparation, good vocabulary, development of style, and mastery of the material will be present in reading a manuscript as in the preparation of a manuscript for memorization. Good writing is never to be despised.

At the same time, the disadvantages are overwhelming. Reading a manuscript, like memorization, often plays up style and downgrades the outline and the ideas. The outline gets buried, and the sense of movement and progression in the speech disappear. The ideas and structure are the important elements of the speech, not the rhetoric— particularly if its style is more literary than oral. The big problem, of course, is that when one reads a speech, one does not establish eye contact with the audience, and thus one loses the opportunity to relate to it directly and spontaneously. Instead, there will be indirectness; and the style

101

itself—especially if literary—will provide its own barrier. Directness cannot be overemphasized. The most effective speaker will be the one who will maintain close contact with the audience. The loss of contact through reading from a text is too high a price to pay.

Most of us as speakers need all of our talents—however modest—working for us all of the time. We cannot say that our ideas and style are so good that we can read a speech and all will listen. We need the support of our ideas, outlines, voice, delivery, eye contact, and so on. For this reason, the most effective way of speaking is, for most people, the extemporaneous method. This manner of speaking is often confused with impromptu, which is speaking without prior preparation. That method is inexcusable for a serious speaker and deserves little or no attention.

The extemporaneous method, on the other hand, takes a great deal of preparation. The focus of this approach is the culmination of the suggestions made thus far in our discussion. The emphasis is upon the central idea, the structure and development of the speech, and effective delivery. There should be a cogent idea, a well-worded thesis, and a clear outline. If anything is memorized or committed to memory it will be the outline and the sequence of ideas. The focus is not on the literary rhetoric, but on the oral style. The speech should be practiced aloud before delivery. In some cases, it is permissible to write it out, but only to be sure that one possesses the vocabulary to handle the ideas. Then the manuscript should be put away. If this extra step of writing out the text can be avoided, and more oral practice substituted for it, it should be done.

For a person new to speaking, or used to writing speeches, this method may at first seem frightening. The language may seem awkward, sentences badly constructed, participles left dangling, infinitives split—all because one is not used to constructing the language for a speech "on one's feet." Repetition may also be part of the learner's problem. Going over the material, then repeating it, staying too long in one place, or generally stumbling may seem to be the plight of a novice speaker who is struggling to speak for the first time in an extemporary mode.

Though it is true that we may get into overly involved sentences, make grammatical errors, stammer a bit, and have long pauses while we try to think of words to come next, the advantages of the method outweigh the disadvantages. For one thing, our style will improve with the challenge. The more speeches we give, the easier it will be for the right words to come. And the language will be oral rather than written style—shorter sentences, simpler words, less abstract and more concrete thoughts. Repetition may not be as bad as we think it is. Laboring a point is distracting, of course, but repeating a good idea is not always unwarranted. Also, what seems like an interminable pause to us may be a great relief to the audience. Further, and above all, the directness and audience rapport the speaker gains through being free of a set format will more than compensate for any disadvantages the method may have.

As to the form of notes the speaker uses on the podium during the speech itself, this will vary from speaker to speaker and makes little difference. Some will use detailed notes, others the basic outline, some very few notes, and some no notes at all. The important question to ask is this: How can I be the most communicative with my audience? Whatever contributes to that end is permissible; whatever hinders communication should be avoided.

In summary, the effective speech needs to have effective delivery. To do so, several principles should be kept in mind:

1. Our voices—whatever their quality—can be improved with work, and practice in this area should be taken as seriously as our dedication in other areas, including our Christian commitment.

2. Special work should be undertaken in order to insure the effective use of the vocal mechanism. Professional help may be needed to gain proper use of the voice. One's own practice can aid the same process.

3. Reading aloud is an indispensable exercise for the effective speaker. It helps with breathing, enunciation, force, volume, expression, and poise.

4. Conversational speaking is the norm for effective speaking, but it is conversation heightened for the speech-event.

5. Our emotions are part of our delivery and should be communicated. Emotion is not the same as emotionalism and should not be thought of negatively.

6. The extemporaneous method of delivery commends itself to the speaker as the most effective all-around method of communicating the speech.

9

Follow the Leader
(Leading a Discussion)

An only half-humorous story is told of a man who ran out of his house and into the midst of an unruly mob in the street exclaiming, "I am your leader. Where are we going?" Though a quip, that story illustrates one extreme of leadership—the leaderless leader. The other extreme is the dominant dictator. Both are to be avoided. A good leader will be neither.

Lay persons who are called upon to speak in various capacities are often called upon to do other things too. Leading discussions, chairing committees, giving reports, and recruiting other leaders are some of the duties that often fall to lay persons. In fact, participating in a discussion as a leader or panel member is not unusual for most persons in the church. The reason is clear: busy and effective persons in one area are usually busy and effective persons in other areas. For our purposes, it is also important to point out that the basic skills needed to prepare and effectively deliver a speech are also implicit in other realms. That is, the principles of communication, public speaking, and persuasion are also prevalent in an area such as leading a group discussion, which is the concern of this chapter. Though group discussion has techniques that need specific emphasis, there is no magic about it. Speech is the basic factor in communication. Though the forms may vary, a skilled leader will function in a verbal context.

To explore the functions of group leadership, it would be well to consider first some of the different groups and settings in which one might be called to operate. Several come to mind at once. One might be asked to lead a discussion at a retreat after a speech has been made, or to chair a committee in the church on plans for a financial campaign. Or, one might lead a group discussing a statement of general church policy, or be requested to address a community organization that is discussing a proposed line of action in regard to better race relations in the community. The list for which good discussion leaders are needed is endless.

The first, if not most important, rule for leading a discussion is preparation. Though leading a group may seem to be no more complicated than sitting around in a circle chatting, an effective leader should not walk into such a setting "cold." His degree of preparation will depend upon the nature of the subject and of the group. In the above examples, the preparation would vary. In leading a discussion after a speech has been made, the preparation could be accomplished in different ways. If the invited speaker has a text for his speech, the discussion leader could look at it before the speech and have time to examine the speech in print. If not, the leader could take careful notes during the speech, use the time between the speech and the discussion to organize the notes, and then formulate the questions, problems, or items that give direction to the discussion.

In the case of chairing a committee in the church on the financial program, one would have plenty of time to assemble the data and talk to the minister and other people who would have direct responsibility for the financial program of the church. In this instance, there would normally be time for thorough preparation prior to the discussion. The same would be true for a discussion on general church policy. Although all members of the group presumably would have copies and had time to read them, the leader faces a special responsibility in needing to master the material in order to be a competent chairperson. The secular organization discussing racial relations would give the leader opportunity to read many materials, national and local, that pertained to the subject. No matter how informed others might be in any given group, the leader should be especially well informed, and should go into the meeting thoroughly at ease with the subject and with the procedures to be followed.

Regardless of the type of discussion to be led, there are two ways in which the leader's preparation takes place. The first is to become familiar with the subject matter to be covered (if this is at all possible). As we have seen, this will vary according to the group, the occasion, and the time available for prior study. The second aspect of leadership is planning the discussion itself, including the way it will unfold. Spontaneity cannot or should not be anticipated or ruled out; nevertheless, the leader should go into most meetings having given some attention to the organization of the discussion.

Occasionally a group will be completely structureless and may not even need a leader—as is characteristic of some informal discussions—but our concern here is with the "chaired" discussion and with the specific responsibilities that accrue to the leader in this case.

Though there are many special areas the leader should be concerned with other than familiarizing himself or herself with the materials of the discussion, several are basic and should not be overlooked. The first should be the introduction of the discussion. The manner of setting the stage for the discussion to follow may vary, but essentially it will have two facets. First, there may be procedural ground-rules outlined. For example, the time limit may be set, and the decision made to proceed through certain questions (or to discuss certain preliminary matters); or the leader may enlist the group's help in establishing both the agenda of that particular discussion and the procedures that will be followed. In the latter case, however, the chances are that the leader will lose control of the discussion.

The second and most important part of the introduction may be setting before the group an introduction of the content of the discussion. This can be dangerous, however; for the leader may consciously or unconsciously say too much and thus undercut the need for the discussion. Too much time might also be taken, or the direction of the discussion predetermined. Nevertheless, the stage may be set for the discussion that follows. In the case of a discussion following a speech, the leader might briefly summarize the thesis of the speaker and then let the discussion develop along the lines of the implications raised by the speech. In another instance, a financial group discussion might begin with the leader setting forth the injunction for raising money (a budget having already been adopted). Even the amount needed might be stated, and the discussion could then proceed along the path of how the church body might raise the funds. In short, the introduction has a function similar to the introduction of a speech. It gets the attention of the group, sets the mood, focuses the attention, and then presents a subject to be investigated.

The leader, having become familiar with the content of the discussion, can proceed by formulating questions that evoke response and keep the discussion moving. Questions have the advantage of being in a form that suggests responses should be forthcoming. The responses, however, do not always have to be in the form of answers. A strong and verbal member of the group may jump immediately to answer the question and assume that that closes the door on other answers. Or, the leader—especially if there are a few awkward moments of silence—may jump in to answer the question that has been tossed out. In either case, the discussion will be deadened, if not stopped. If a question is answered too quickly by an aggressive participant, the leader can move to others, stating, "Now what do some of the rest of you think?" Or, in the case of the awkward silence, the dead moments may not be felt as painfully if they are thought of as times that people are thinking. The leader may reformulate the question in a better way, or if he or she knows the group well enough, may direct the question to some specific person.

Questions, it must be remembered, are not always phrased so as to be answered; they may be intended to further discussion. The group dealing with church financial matters may need a question like "What are some of the ways that money could be raised in our church?" There could be no one answer capable of stopping the discussion. In fact, there could be many responses given to the question, without exhausting the subject. In such a case, it may be necessary for the leader to move the discussion along before the group gets bogged down on only one question.

It cannot be emphasized too strongly that the leader is just that, a leader, and should not dominate the discussion. Leading, being involved in, and keeping the discussion moving along are all parts of the task. But talking too much, answering the questions, cutting off others, and failing to listen are qualities that will cause both the leader and the group to fail. The good leader is, in a sense, both in and out of the discussion. His or her views can be presented, but it is imperative that the views of others be aired.

If the leader must hold in check his or her own tendency to talk (which may be natural since the same kinds of persons who enjoy speaking are often good leaders), the leader's most important task in the group may be to curtail the persons in the group who are overtalkative. This can be done several ways. One has been mentioned. If a person seems too ready to talk at every turn, then the leader can move on by enlisting another's participation. Or, if a person tends to talk too long, a gentle interruption can be made by suggesting that someone else is attempting to speak. Often the group itself will do its own ''policing,'' by handling the one who tries to dominate. They might interrupt, move the subject in another direction, and sometimes directly suggest that the discussion is being dominated and others need a chance. If this latter is done in good spirit without creating ill will, then the leader should not try to interfere with the group's interaction. The overtalkative person may have certain needs that are being met by trying to dominate the group. While the domination of the group by anyone needs to be curtailed, the group's solidarity and efficiency should not be marred by pointless hostility.

As serious a problem as the outspoken participant may be, the shy, withdrawn, quiet person may be even more difficult. One should face the fact, however, that some people are retiring—for whatever reason—and are not going to say much. They may be good listeners, may not necessarily be withdrawn because they are unhappy, and may be tremendously interested and alert, but they simply will not participate. The leader ought not to punish himself or herself because responses have not been elicited; he should accept the fact that some people will never say much, and go on with the discussion.

Others may be quiet, though, because they are intimidated by more vocal and stronger personalities. They may want to talk, but they are too shy, too unaggressive, or too fearful of conflict to take the risk. Therefore, they "clam up," are easily hurt, and often leave the group frustrated. With these persons, the leader has a special responsibility. He or she can encourage them to speak, call on them by name, run interference for them by feeding them questions, affirming their points and urging them to expand their ideas.

The most difficult person to handle in the discussion group may be oneself. We earlier alluded to the fact that the same communication skills that make a person effective in speaking before a group will be those that make him successful in leading a group. The same is true for leadership.

The person who is effective in communication in one area will most likely be effective in others. When these communicative skills and leadership abilities combine in the leader of the group, domination can easily be the result. As suggested earlier, the leader needs to be careful of becoming a dictator. At the same time, the leader's own views can and should be expressed; for he or she is also part of the group. Indeed, the group leader's prior preparation may make him the best informed among all the discussants.

How does one participate creatively as a leader without dominating the discussion? For one thing, the introduction to the discussion, while not predetermining its content and direction, gives the leader a creative opportunity to set the style of the discussion and to provide information at that critical moment when it can be most helpful. Further, if the leader formulates questions along the way, he can introduce new ideas and fresh insights and thus always be ready as an important resource person. Or, the leader may be asked directly to speak to an issue. This he or she should do without reservation. The leader should also feel free to speak as a member of the group at the opportune time, but with restraint. The summary at the end of the discussion provides the leader with a great opportunity to bring together the strands of the discussion, including the leader's ideas, and then to tie the whole period together with a creative impact. In short, for much of the time, the leader of a group discussion will be like a policeman directing traffic, but there will also be opportunities for him to be a part of the parade.

As mentioned earlier, timing is as important in a discussion as it is in a speech. There is, of course, the overall period of time set for the discussion, which must be adhered to as with a speech. The leader should be conscious of time without seeming rushed. He must keep one eye on the clock, to keep the discussion moving, yet not inhibit discussion by obviously pushing it along. Within the discussion, the leader will attempt to avoid lingering on one point too long without being abrupt. This can be done easily enough by the leader's suggesting another question or simply asking that the discussion raise another question. One must be careful not to interrupt a person in the middle of making a point, and one should also be on guard not to leave an important point or issue unresolved. This does not mean, however, that the leader should expect to cover everything.

Timing is also important. A leader may be too anxious to fill an interval of "dead space" in the discussion; for the silence may indicate only a collective pause for reflection. The leader must be patient with these kinds of breaks, and step in only after a while to move things along or to rephrase the previous question. Pausing in a discussion, as in a speech, may give a good rhythm to the discussion if it is not prolonged. The other extreme would be "lagging." If the discussion is slow, filled with interminable pausing, and little is being accomplished, then time is being wasted and the leader needs to act to keep it moving. The makeup of the group may affect the movement and the effectiveness of the discussion, of course, but the leader needs to be alert to a real slowdown, and to what it will take to get the group back on the track and moving toward its desired end.

Throughout this chapter our assumption has been that

group discussion develops along the lines of a brief introduction, a series of questions, and a summary conclusion. Obviously, groups are dynamic, not static, and there are as many ways to proceed as there are number of groups and varieties of personalities who make up the groups. Still, the principles enunciated in this chapter are applicable to all groups and leaders, and the basic skills outlined are applicable to a variety of discussions. Several other types should be indicated in addition, however. One is a problem-solving type of discussion. In this case, instead of moving through the discussion with a series of questions, the problem-solving group begins with a specific problem (such as the finance picture in a local church) and through the ensuing discussion, attempts to arrive at a solution for that particular problem. Extemporaneous questions, free discussion, specific factual input, or small-group reporting are the ways such a group performs. This kind of a group would be task-oriented, moving toward a conclusion that would be specific in its application.

Another type would follow a series of points or propositions. A service club committee might be discussing the various ways it could use its surplus funds during the coming year. The discussion would be a series of alternatives and options—each one demanding time for clarification and exploration. The goal might not be a concrete resolution of the subject matter, but simply a thorough airing of it. From this particular discussion others would most likely follow.

And, of course, there is the freewheeling discussion—seemingly going nowhere—that is, nevertheless, appropriate on some occasions. A speech at a lay retreat might raise an issue such as an ethical response to war, sex, race, or nuclear energy. The discussion could move dynamically over a wide area. Such discussions can be fruitful for getting the group involved, but they may call for the leader to be sensitive and wise enough to stay on top of the entire process.

Whatever the form of the discussion, however, the leader will need to remember certain principles that pertain to the conduct of any group meeting.

In summary:

1. The skills of communication are as basic to leading a group as they are to public speaking, classroom teaching, personal interview, or report making.

2. Whatever the nature of the group to be led, there can be no substitute for adequate preparation. The leader must take responsibility for being adequately prepared whatever the situation.

3. The good leader will need to be sensitive to the careful balance between *leading* and *listening.* Without the former, the group will meander and be formless; without the latter, the leader will dominate, and it will be a speech occasion.

4. The leader must be skillful in handling members of the group, especially in drawing out the quieter ones and carefully curbing those who would take over the discussion.

5. There are various ways groups may proceed due to their assigned purpose. Some will develop discussion through questions, others through stated propositions; some will solve specific problems; and others will be unstructured. The leader will adapt to the various types, remembering the principles that underlie all.

6. The leader should be free to express his or her own opinion—even to be an advocate—but should be careful not to abdicate the role of leader to become only a discussant. It is better to contribute to the discussion as a resource person and an enabler than as a participant.

10

Even the Kitchen Sink
(Other Speech Occasions)

We have all heard the expression, "Everything but the kitchen sink." That old cliche has been applied to all sorts of things, all the way from soup to speeches. In a sense, this final chapter includes the kitchen sink; for it is very clear that the lay person has an amazing number of opportunities to be involved in all sorts of speech functions.

The busy minister who speaks at conferences, service clubs, and banquets will spend the bulk of speech time on sermons—or should. The lay person, however, will be called upon for a variety of speeches and oral performances that will run the gamut of a word of personal witness to a formal speech in front of a sizable audience. Our purpose here is to gather together some of these various experiences and make suggestions for handling them effectively.

One of the major forms of speaking in front of groups has to do with giving reports. Part of the price we pay for a highly organized society is the accumulation of data, figures, balance sheets, statistics, and reports. What is more, someone has to tell someone else what they all mean. That job often falls to the same kind of articulate lay person who also will be giving speeches and serving as a leader in the church. How do we go about taking a report and making it come alive?

First of all, as in all other forms of public speaking, the primary concern is preparation. If one has to give a report from a printed document that has tables, numbers, and statistics, as well as summaries, conclusions, and suggestions for action, then the speaker should take the opportunity to do prior study. Hopefully, most reports will be of this nature, though occasionally one may have to take over after a committee has met and make an impromptu report to a larger body. Usually, though, the report maker is working with material of the former sort, and the preparation involves several stages. First, he should read the material very carefully to make sure he understands it clearly. Points that are not clear should be gone over, looked up elsewhere, or submitted to the opinion of an expert. For example, suppose the report concerned a retirement home that the church or a group of churches owned. Part of the report would likely contain a balance sheet of the home's operating expenses during the current year. As the report maker, you might have little trouble understanding the report in general, but you still might not be too clear on how to read and interpret the balance sheet. Part of the preparation, then, would be to ask an accountant in the church to help interpret the figures.

After reading the report carefully and checking the points not understood, it would be advisable to take notes on the highlights of the report that will be the main content of the presentation. At this stage of constructing the report, one is going through the same steps as in building a speech. Indeed, much of the well-presented report should sound like a well-presented speech. The differences, though, may be significant, and they certainly need special attention and emphasis.

One of the most important differences is the care with which statistics are presented. Numbers can be both boring and forgettable. In many reports, however, they are of the utmost importance. Therefore, they must be made memorable and arresting. There are several ways numbers can come alive. One way would be to put the numbers in a more striking form. For example, instead of saying "Our retirement home has 398 applications a year for admission," a better way would be to round off the number. "Our retirement home processes around 400 applications per year." Four hundred would be easier to remember.

Another way would be to take numbers and make them into percentages. Using the same example, the speaker might say, "Of the approximately 400 applications per year, our home is able to take only 25 percent, or 100." The percentages and the fraction will support and reinforce the original figures. Comparisons would be another way of making the statistics stand out in people's minds. One could say, for example, "Our private home, though without state support, has been given a higher rating than any other public home in this state." That comparison would be remembered long after the meeting is over. Sometimes, though, the numbers and tables cannot be reduced to startling percentages or dramatic comparisons. If that is true and they are important for the report to be made, then the speaker can use visual aids. An overhead projector, or, most easily, a blackboard can project the important figures so the audience can see them. It is easier to remember the spoken information about statistics if it can be reinforced by the visual. If the audience has in its hands a copy of the same report that the speaker has, those sections, numbers, or statistics that are especially important can be underlined by the audience even as the speaker highlights them in his oral presentation. Certainly visual demonstration demands thorough preparation, but it is an effective way of dramatizing content that might otherwise be dismissed as boring.

Now let us turn to another type of speech situation that often confronts the lay person—a speech of introduction. Here a speaker will be asked to perform a function that on the surface seems easy and obvious, but as a matter of fact, is prone to receiving slipshod and ineffective treatment. Some attention to preparation, though, can make a tremendous difference in both the introduction itself and, more importantly, in aiding the speaker whom you will present. There are several things to remember in preparing a speech of introduction.

The first is that the introduction should be brief. Though it would be difficult to set a specific time limit for an introduction, the speaker should err on the side of brevity rather than length. The shorter the introduction, the more compact, and the more thought given to it, the more impact it will have. Brevity is the first rule, but closely related to it is the strong reminder that the speech of introduction introduces yet another person. How many speeches have you heard in which the introducer rambled, took too long, and, above all, talked about himself. It was as if it were his occasion. The focus should be on the person who follows. Getting the person before the audience—setting the scene and creating a mood for the speech—this is what should be kept clearly in the mind as an introduction is prepared. The mood refers to the necessity of having the tone of the introduction fit the tone of the speech. A funny introduction would not normally precede a speech on a somber theme. Preparation, again, is the key. Learn all you can about the person you are to introduce. If she or he has a biographical statement or a publicity brochure, study those and take from them only the important points. Do not tell the speaker's life story. In addition, pick out those items of background that have a bearing on the speech to follow. If the title of the speech is available, give that too. In the end, if you have singled out the important aspects of the speaker's life, provided some background for the speech, announced the title—all with grace and brevity—then the introduction can be called successful.

Another speaking role that lay persons are often asked to perform is master of ceremonies. Youth banquets, men's clubs, service club luncheons, special family nights, or athletic dinners are some of the many diverse functions at which someone is needed to preside, introduce guests, and chair the program. It is difficult to be too specific about rules covering every occasion, because they all differ; and the style of the master of ceremonies will adapt his or her approach to a specific situation. Normally, though, these affairs are lighthearted and call for a humorous touch.

Humor is a very elusive quality and deserves more attention than we have given thus far. In connection with the role of master of ceremonies, a discussion of humor seems most natural. Though not absolutely required, a sense of humor will put the emcee more at ease in his role. Humor is not just telling jokes and laughing at them. It is more, and it is deeper. Humor is the ability to stand outside oneself and laugh at human frailties. Humorous people can usually make fun of themselves, tell stories well, and relate warmly to others on the program.

Not everyone can handle humor. It is like the old story about the New Englander who was asked if Puritans could dance. The response was, "Some can. Some can't." Humor is the same way. Nothing is more ludicrous than a person attempting to be funny to whom it does not come naturally. Our authentic selves will be revealed when we come before an audience, as we have seen. To try to be something we are not will be revealing. On the other hand, the person who is good with humor needs to be careful. It can go to his head, and having tasted success in this area, he can find it hard to turn it off. It should be handled with restraint. In a religious speech, for example, it may sometimes be out of place. And, in the situation under consideration, the master of ceremonies, the circumstances would be helped by humor. As with the person making an introduction, however, the object is not to feature the master of ceremonies, but to feature the program itself and those who are participating in it.

Here, then, is the focus for the master of ceremonies. He or she can be clever, funny, arresting, or entertaining. These would be all to the good. But the primary interest must be the program. It could be an athletic banquet that consists of various coaches presenting awards to their teams, followed by a guest speaker. The toastmaster would want to see that the program moves along, that the coaches are introduced

122

effectively, and that the guest speaker is presented to the crowd in a courteous and appropriate way. If all of this can be done subtly, with a deft touch of humor, with timing and good taste, then the chances for success are good.

Another kind of communication event is the after-dinner speech, which is somewhat like being the master of ceremonies except that the roles are reversed. In the former, you may be called upon to introduce the speaker as part of your duties. In the latter, you will be the speaker. However, the context for both roles will be similar. In most cases, the after-dinner speech also calls for a light touch; it is often humorous and informal in tone. What was said about humor before is appropriate here. The person who can handle humor well will have an advantage in after-dinner speaking. Those who cannot, will do better to concentrate on what they can do well. Telling a joke at the beginning of the speech to get attention or establish rapport will be ineffective unless it comes easily to the speaker. If the joke does not lead naturally into the speech, it will show itself to the audience as an obvious attention-getting device.

Apart from humor, though, the after-dinner speech will be similar to any other type. One of the most tempting fallacies is that a lighthearted, humorous, or informal speech needs very little preparation. On the contrary, many well-known comedians or comic actors find their extemporaneous roles terribly demanding. What seem like tossed-off lines, ad libs, and informal asides may have been thought through very carefully. So, the first word of advice to the after-dinner speaker is the same as to any other speaker—prepare. The speech should be given careful work, sometimes researched, notes taken, and structured with a beginning and an end. In other words, the after-dinner speech *is* a speech. It should not consist of off-the-cuff remarks. So, preparing the speech will be the first order of business. Then, attention should be given to delivery. That should be informal, conversational, and direct. For most speakers this would mean few or no notes, and certainly not a manuscript. With attention to preparation, there is no reason the after-dinner speech cannot be done with competence and even with flair by the average lay speaker.

Another very familiar role for the public speaker is that of a committee chairperson. In many ways, chairing a committee is similar to leading a discussion. There are differences, however. All of the qualities of a good discussion leader would be present. In addition, the chairperson should be absolutely impartial as a presider. There may be times when the leader wishes to speak directly to a point as an advocate, but he should either ask permission to do so or turn over the chair to someone else while speaking. Normally, even though the committee may be small, the chairperson should maintain general parliamentary rules of order. Good communication, fairness, sensitivity to the participants, firmness with those who wish to take over the meeting, and consciousness of those who need encouragement to participate are all qualities that will serve well the leader of a committee, group, or discussion.

The various areas of communication and public speaking we have considered in this chapter by no means exhaust the possibilities for the effective communicator. The list is endless—funeral eulogies, personal witness and testifying, orations at civic celebrations, and many other occasions at which one might participate in some visible and verbal way. Our purpose has been, on the one hand, to describe some of the most important ones, and on the other hand, to outline the basic principles that underlie all of our communicative experiences. Indeed, that has been the purpose of the entire book—to enable the lay person to become more aware of what it takes to be an effective communicator.

The effective communicator will be called upon to function in a variety of ways, as this chapter has indicated.

To summarize:

1. Reports can be given clarity, even excitement, if it is remembered that preparation is the key and that figures and statistics can come alive when they are placed in an unusual or dramatic light.

2. Introductions of other people may be one of the sloppiest types of oral addresses. These can, however, be executed effectively if they are kept brief and if they focus on the person being introduced and not on the introducer.

3. A master of ceremonies or toastmaster needs to focus on the program and keep his or her own role subordinate. However, if the role can be performed with humor and a sense of timing and good taste, then the role will have been performed well.

4. The after-dinner speaker will also be aided by humor if it comes naturally. The speech should be carefully prepared, usually kept brief, and delivered conversationally with natural directness.

5. The chairperson of a committee or an official meeting should be fair, impartial, and sensitive to others. Parliamen-

tary rules should be mastered if one is called upon to perform this function regularly.

  6. All speech occasions have within them certain common principles of communication. A person who learns to speak well can perform competently in all these various areas.

No matter what the situation or occasion, the lay person can be an effective speaker. If he or she takes the job seriously, follows the principles of good communication in this and other books, and gives any specific assignment adequate thought and preparation, then the speech occasion should be welcomed. To hold an audience—even for a moment—"in the palm of your hand" is an exhilarating experience. Or, to feel that you have been able to put your ideas across to other people can be exciting and rewarding. Above all, to be able to work closely with others, to see communication take place within the group and know that you have had a part in it, certainly brings fulfillment. Indeed, we should realize that God's gift of the human voice, words, and the power to communicate may be the greatest of all our gifts. Knowing this and training ourselves to be able to respond to others effectively should challenge us to accept the role of communicator whenever the opportunity presents itself.

126